A Youth Basketball
Coaching Guide

A Youth Basketball Coaching Guide

Danford Chamness

Writers Club Press
San Jose New York Lincoln Shanghai

A Youth Basketball Coaching Guide

Writers Club Press
an imprint of iUniverse.com, Inc.

For information address:
iUniverse.com, Inc.
620 North 48th Street, Suite 201
Lincoln, NE 68504-3467
www.iuniverse.com

ISBN: 0-595-13685-0

Printed in the United States of America

To all of the children who dream of the NBA & WNBA.

Contents

Below Basket at Low Post, fake, pivot & put it up.
At midpost, fake, pivot and put it up.
At high post, fake, pivot, break and put it up.
Fundamental Rebounding Exercise & Drill.

Basic Pick and Roll.
Shuffle Cut-misdirection by feint.
Slice around post-Single break to lane.
Slice around post-Two above high post crisscross.
Backdoor by Forward.
Slice play: Guard & Forward on strong side.
Clear out for Pivot Man.
Rotational Offensive Pattern:
Jump Ball Tactics
The Offensive Box Formation.
The Deffensive 1-1-1-2 Formation.
Do's and Don'ts:

Forward

This book was written expressly for you who are coaching children in basketball. We stress how to teach children this complex game and to have fun doing it. The book covers all facets of the game from "how to" dribbling to strategies and tactics.

When coaching children it should be a fun experience for everyone, for you, for the parents, and most important of all, for the children. As a coach, we cover the teaching attitude and methods. We always keep in mind that these are children, and the game is for the kids and not for the adults. Winning isn't everything, but learning to play well and wanting to win is.

We have taken the children from first grade through the eighth grade and broken them into four categories. In each category we discuss the players needs and abilities, what they are capable of in both the physical and emotion sense, and their limitations. We have also defined the coach's role, the parent's role and the player's role.

We primarily stress how to teach children this complex game and to have fun doing it. The book covers all facets of the game from "how to" dribble to strategies and tactics. In the area of "set" plays we develop the basic plans and allow you and your team to build on them. We didn't intend this book for high school and beyond, but the basics apply anywhere the game is played.

Understand that the team is a composite of three important elements. The coaching staff, the parents and the players of the team. Leadership of this composite rests upon the coaching staff. It has the responsibility for directing and maintaining the program from its beginning until its end.

As a coach you are building attitudes and memories with these youngsters that they will carry with them for a lifetime. You are the first to give them an identity away from home or school. You have made them a member of a team, and assigned them a responsible position on the team.

This is their first step to independence and self reliance. And you are helping them take that first step. Leading a youngster into his or her own identity is the birth of their character to come. There is not enough praise that can be given to you for your selfless efforts to train our young people.

I always remain aware that these kids are the hope of all of our tomorrow's. And by doing a good job with them early, you have given more to their future than you realize.

Thank you for your participation.

Acknowledgments

The "National Youth Sports Coaches Association" was developed to train coaches in the techniques and methods of coaching young people. It is coaching specific. I am proud to be a member of this organization, and I highly recommend that you consider becoming one yourself.

NYSCA

National Youth Sports Coaching Association
2050 Vista Parkway, West Palm Beach, FL 33411
(561) 684-1141, (800) 729-2057, Fax (561) 684-2546
E-Mail: nays @ nays.org
Web Site: Intp:/www.nays.org

Becoming a NYSCA certified coach does not indicate that you are qualified in the sense of a paid coach on the high school, college, or professional level. By virtue of your attending the NYSCA Training Certification Program conducted by a qualified Clinician. NYSCA Headquarters certifies that you have been trained in your responsibilities to children in sports specifically.

The City of Burbank, Parks and Recreation Sports Department is an outstanding example of what a well organized group can do. I have had the good fortune of working as a volunteer coach for this department for a number of years. With limited facilities and multiple sports in progress at any one time, they perform pure magic when it comes to scheduling games and practice sessions.

The city through it's meticulous selection of staffing personnel has managed to attract an outstanding number of dedicated people. I thank them for all of the support they have given to the coaches in their efforts to train the children in this community.

Chapter 1

Coaches Corner

So you're ready to coach? Great! This book is dedicated to you and the member's of your team. And as a coach you are more than just a trainer of young athletes in the fine art of this chosen sport, but their mentor and teacher. This carries a lot of responsibility. Not just the idea of building a winning team, but the molding of character and creating a firm foundation of good sportsmanship.

Your own goal should be to have fun teaching these youngsters how to play this most difficult of all sports. Make it a point to bring your sense of humor to every practice session or game. Basketball requires a wider range of skills than any other single group sport. You've probably not thought about that. But it's a very intricate and complex game played at speed, both in body and mind.

Learn to laugh at yourself and laugh with your team. Have realistic expectations about what your team can accomplish. Share their expectations about what they think they can do. Think more of "we" than "me" and you'll become that winning coach you want to be. All of this effort is for the children, not for the adults.

As their coach, you are responsible for scheduling all practices, getting uniforms, setting game dates, handling the players rotation roster, first aid on the court, player releases and a hundred other details. Don't expect others to appreciate the amount of time and effort you will expend. You are a coach! How well you organize your program is very important. You must also have the most current rules publication available to you because almost every year, some rule changes.

As the coach, you also become the team's trainer. The Training side is when you are teaching the fundamental skills required to play the game, it's the "how to" phase. How to dribble, how to pass, how to put the ball up, how to rebound and so on. This phase does not include practice games or scrimmage games, it is specifically training.

Under training, you will run practice drills, and give instructions which assist the player in learning "how to". Depending on the age and experience of your new team, the amount of "how to" may vary considerably.

Training for the younger players will require more training time in the basic fundamentals than the older boys. You assess the skill level early on with your team by having them perform the most basic skills required to play the game. Once the teams basic skill level is determined, you either raise or lower the basic skill level of drills to be practiced.

At this point you must develop realistic goals you should hope to achieve with the players. Form a schedule of how and when you should reach a particular goal. Once an overall plan is put together, you are organized. Now you have a means of measuring yourself and your teams success. Having a reference point for achievement is as important to you as it is to the team.

Making your training time count is based upon how you prepare the training program and the amount of detail you put into it. Always have a plan in advance, then follow it. Those youngsters who are slower to learn than the others will of course require more of your personal attention. Give it with a smile.

When we are coaching youngsters, consider boys from 6 to 15 as being in this category. They arrive filled with hope and expectation to improve their skills and to have fun. Don't forget the word play in "play basketball". Leave the furrowed brow, pulled down mouth and scornful voice at the door.

As a coach, you are the leader, trainer, booster, supporter, manager, and a host of many positive things. To be all of that requires constant monitoring of yourself and your reactions. It's a darn tough job. All of us have reflex reactions that at times can be very inappropriate to a situation at hand. Often times holding these in check is difficult if not almost impossible.

Reflex is a conditioned response which can cause us to say or do something we will later regret. Just remember, you can't un-ring the bell. Some people call this overreaction, and it is. That old business about counting to ten first, really holds true, so use it. Like it or not, you are the authority figure. Always conduct yourself as such. Don't smoke, use smokeless tobacco or profanity in front of the team. Set an example you would prefer your son or daughter to have.

Now that I've mentioned your son or daughter, it's a good time to consider whether or not you're coaching your own child. If that is the case, there are some guidelines you must consider. Consider first if your child wants you to be his or her coach. Some children do not want to be coached by a parent because the relation is to close to their daily routine.

Next, review your own reasons and interest for coaching your child. Are you attempting to make him or her a "star" by giving the child preferential treatment? If that be the case, you're off on the wrong foot. That causes a lot of conflict among other the players on the team, and with their parents. Your child is then subjected to a negative backlash from the other players.

Another problem we run into when coaching our own children is we sometimes expect more from them than their counterparts. This is unfair to the child. Let the child grow at it's own rate. Allow him or her the freedom of being like any other kid on the team. Do not compare your child's accomplishments to those of others.

Don't single your child out for his performance any differently than you do with any other team member. Try to keep the playing field level for all participants. Maintain an even balance when you administer discipline.

Team Discipline only requires that you be firm and even handed with your directions and your coaching attitude. You are not running a marine barracks. Children lose focus during practice or the drills after a short period of time, that's normal. Don't allow that to irritate you, if it does, give the kids and yourself a break.

Let's talk about the kids for a moment. They are pretty much blank pages for you. They come in a variety of sizes, maturity levels, skill levels, and of playing experience. Some have good hand-eye coordination and some don't. Some may have physical disabilities such as asthma, epilepsy, shortness of breath, hard of hearing, or eye problems which are not obvious by looking at them.

Take any age group, for instance 10 to 11 year old boys, their abilities and sizes will run the gambit. However, there are several common denominators among all youngsters. Their vulnerability, their wanting to please you, and their need for positive reinforcement. Simple achievements build their self esteem. They need you to be their positive booster.

If your kids are lucky, you will create a sports sanctuary where they learn to play the game and have fun doing so. Having fun is the key to good coaching. Make it fun for the players and yourself. No youngster learns well under harsh instruction or by ridicule from either parents or others. Also consider that you have little if any information regarding your wards, other than they are interested in learning to play the game.

Take into account that you know nothing about their outside environment or inner family relationships. Young people have many stressful conditions imposed on them by family expectations, school and their own social group. Some may come from very repressive home environments, some may be mentally and emotionally abused, others can get far worse treatment.

You have no way of knowing what goes on where and with whom in your charge. In pointing this out, I'm urging you to consider first the players need for your booster ability. Treat him/her fairly and calmly when giving your instructions. Never get into an argument with a child. The moment you do, you have lost. Simply repeat the instruction and move on.

There's a good reason why I've taken this time to point out abuse. Child abuse can be anything from indifference and neglect to murder. Hard words but true. It exists on a wide variety of levels and you as a coach should be aware of it. Take for instance the act of expressing your delight over a players successful performance on the court. High five's, shoulder slaps, hair ruffling or shoulder squeezes are affectionate displays of caring and approval.

And these have a place in the sports arena, they demonstrate acceptance and improve self worth. However, never, and I repeat never pat, rub or touch the kids below the belt. This can easily be misunderstood by him, her and others.

A player expects fairness from the coach when playing schedules re assigned. No boy wants to sit on the bench while the others are in the game. Players then reflect upon themselves that you don't feel they are good enough to play. And they assume that you, without saying a word have shown your feelings about his playing ability. If he can recognize, and should, that you are being both fair to him as an individual and the team as a whole, you've got a happy camper.

An example of kids thinking can go like this: The boy had a great game, everything he did worked. It was the best he had ever played but the team lost the game. Because the team lost did not make him unhappy because he was happy with how he played. Conversely the boy played a terrible game, nothing worked that he tried but the team won. How do you think he felt about himself? He felt good because the team won.

Winning isn't everything. Losing isn't everything. Playing the game well and wanting to win is everything. Never make too much out of a game lost. Instead have them see it as a learning experience, discuss what adjustments you as a team can make to improve your win/loss performance. Do let the kids know that you are with them and behind them all the way. When you win, you all win, when you lose, you all lose.

You don't have to dictate everything to them. Let them participate in what the team is doing. Encourage the working relationship between the team and you as the coach. Keep an open mind on suggestions and ideas from your team. Let the players arrive at your observation, then confirm it.

Coaching really starts when you begin scrimmages and practice games. And as in a real game, you call a time out, form the team around you and go over what you want to see done. You will have setbacks in the sense that you may have practiced an in bounding exercise and the moment the players are in a practice game, it goes out the window.

That is the time when you call a time out, and calmly go over it verbally with the players. When instruction is given during play then it will stick. Conduct your coaching during practice games in the same manner you will use during a league game.

The more advanced and skilled your players or team becomes, the easier your job gets. Let's examine that thought for a moment. When you are coaching a young team that is just developing it's skills, you are looking primarily at the fundamental mistakes the players are making. You begin listing in your mind the things you will have to emphasize in training.

The poorest player will set the pace for what you must teach in fundamentals. If you're a hell bent for election, gotta win coach, you may find that this will stress you out. Never point a finger at a player for what he's done wrong, remember that when you do, you have three fingers pointing back at you. You adjust your training.

Here again is that philosophy of don't scold. A player may have made a poor choice in what he did, but scolding won't undo the mistake. Both you and the team must accept the reality that mistakes do happen, and they are okay. You simply emphasize what you would like to have done instead of what was done.

This approach makes the team feel is supported by you, instead of scrutinized by you. Build from the positive things your players are doing well. Ring in the reins a little on the "must win" thinking. Direct the team's efforts and let them experiment and have fun. Having fun and bonding with their teammates will develop the winning team for you and them.

Every team you will coach, whether very young or young adult, will develop a bond among themselves. Their shared experience in working towards a common goal is a coalition of individuals. You will be watching this bond form as they share the playing experience.

Once this has begun to take shape, you must consider more closely how you either correct or reprimand your individual players. From within their bond, you are the outsider. Sure, you are the coach, but not a member of the team. Kids are like rope, you can lead them, pull them along, but you can't push them very well. This brings up fraternization with the players. You are the authority figure, they are not your buddies and don't try to make it so.

Don't start saying to them, "C'mon Buddy you can do it." That's well intended, but not good from the separateness you should maintain as an instructing coach. I don't wish to belabor this point, but refer to them by their names which keeps everything on an even keel. They should refer to you as coach, or mister, or misses and not by your first name. We, as coaches must stand apart in order to get the response we want from them, for them.

During a game, don't make comments to individual players about what they are doing or not doing while they are on the court. When you single out a player, you may embarrass him without meaning to. Respect the coaches bench and its regulations. If you have a player who is not doing what you have requested of him, send in a sub and have him report to you on the bench. Conduct your business with him privately, then return him to the game.

If the team is not doing what you've asked them to do. Call a time out and review what it is you need them to do. This is conducted in the presence of all team members without anyone being excluded. It's a matter of fairness and consideration. Do corrections in a positive and reinforcing way. No scolding. Explain as clearly as possible the changes you are looking for and do it with a smile.

If you are coaching a team of good player's. You don't have to look at basic performance mistakes, because they don't make them. You are now in the process of building teamwork. The longer a good team plays together as a team, the more proficient they become in using picks, screens, cuts, give and goes, etc. At this coaching level you are teaching your team how to improve and implement strategies and tactics. Therefore during the game, you are looking for strategies and tactics to help them win.

How do you handle an unruly parent who is shouting at the players on the court during the game? At the quarter break or half time break, take the time to thank the parents for their enthusiasm and remind them of their code of responsibility. Do it calmly and quietly and with a smile. If a parent is admonishing his own child, ask him to help the team by taking some of his extra time to work with his kid to improve his performance. Always try to enlist the parent in a positive way to gain the participation you want.

Now that you are the coach, let's look at what this entails other than being the teams trainer and provider. You should keep a first aid kit available at all times during practice and games. Ice packs are almost always in demand for bangs and bruises, with Band-Aid running a close second.

A coach is responsible;
For teaching the fundamentals of the game.
For creating a good learning environment.
For treating each child fairly.
For individual training needs.
For each child's personal safety.
For each child's safety from others abuse.
For setting a good example.
For creating a team environment.
For building players self esteem.
For encouragement and player fun.

For having patience with the children.
For the parents behavior during a game.
For the players behavior during a game.

A coach has the right;

To cooperation from the parents.
To cooperation from the player.
To cooperation from the league.
To bench a player for inappropriate behavior.
To suspend a player from play.
To not accept a problem player on the team.
To assign his players to their positions.
To have adequate practice facilities.
To fairness in scheduling with the league.

One last note, during a league game or when a number of people are in attendance, only allow your team to use the restrooms when all of the players go together. Keep them together at all times for their own individual safety. Make sure all players are picked up after the game or practice and never leave one behind alone. If you have a player who is waiting for someone to pick them up, you wait with them.

Chapter 2

Players Bench

The youngsters coming into the basketball program want a place where they can play with others like themselves and practice whatever skills they have. Usually they arrive with a great deal of interest about the sport and an attitude about their own ability. However the majority of youngsters are shy and don't want to be singled out to do things which they may not do well.

Yet, they all want to fit in with the others in your program. Each player wants an opportunity to do what he does best, or thinks he does best. He expects the coach to recognize his skills and abilities and instruct him in how to improve them. He expects to be included in all of the activities fairly.

A coach may want a player to be more aggressive on the court. The younger the player, the less physically aggressive he will be. Younger players confuse aggressiveness with hostility, and they do not want to become hostile and lose the fun of the game. No young player wants to be an object of hostility either.

Players prior to the age of puberty are looking at the sport for fun. Players after reaching puberty look at the sport as a way to establish an identity. Young players share interest and involvement. Older players share the same interest and involvement but bring another dimension when seeking identity. In overall respect, all players are wanting to have fun with the game and all of them should.

All players regardless of age seek leadership from adults and coaches. All players want acceptance and recognition. All layers want to play in the game. Some boys are seeking a haven away from their outside environment. A place where they fit. A player expects fairness from the coach when playing schedules are assigned. No boy wants to sit on the bench while the others are in the game.

No player wants to either be made the subject of scrutiny nor to be ignored. During a scrimmage or a game, he expects leadership from the coach in how to best play the game. He is more than willing to follow directions if they are explained in a way which he can understand. Most players feel that if they work hard in practice, do their best as directed, should have the right to play in the game.

This is a players fairness doctrine that should be adhered to. No player is looking to be the fair hair boy or girl, and resents it if there appears to be someone else who is. Boys and girls in the sport find their own place among their peers. It is a place of comfort for them to play from in the team.

Player's Rights & Responsibilities:
A player has the right;
To fairness and respect.
To have fun learning and playing.
To not be ridiculed or harshly scolded.
To make mistakes without punishment.
To a fair amount of playing time on court.

To encouragement for effort.
To protection from abuse by others.
To a safe environment.

A player is responsible;

For attending practices.
For attending the game.
For trying To make a learning effort.
For good conduct on court.
For cooperating with others.
For following directions.
For letting the coach know if he is ill.
For staying with the team at all times.
For asking permission to leave the team.

Chapter 3

Parents Expectations

Parents expect their children to be taught how to play their game of choice while having fun. They expect the coach to be thoughtful, considerate, kind and fair to their prize possession. Parents who involve their young children in sports do so for a variety of reasons. First they want their children to have fun in sports, and group activities.

Parents want their youngsters to acquire self esteem and confidence and to learn the values of good sportsmanship. They want their kids to build a network of friends and enjoy an activity which in the future may guide them away from trouble. All of this is as it should be, and it is also the coaches focus as well.

Parents sometimes have unrealistic expectations about their child's ability to master the basics of the game. They often expect to much from their youngsters. These expectations should be tempered with the realization that they are only children. We have a situation where kids are playing at grown up games. Some children will learn quicker than others and some will be slower than the rest. So what! Parents must let the kids have their play time.

All parents want their children to perform well. When they don't, they get disappointed with their children, the team and the coaches. Not a good thing to have happen. They should never be unhappy over kids trying to play this game as best they can. When the parent gets unhappy with their child's, or the children's performance, their kid feels defeated by not living up to their expectations of him. This spoils it for the child.

Some things a parent should never do.

Never ridicule one of the team members lack of ability to play well to your child. By bad rapping another players deficiencies to your child, only makes him defensive about "his" team.

Never take your coach to task in front of the team. You may not know all you should about either playing the game or coaching it. Never assume that you know why a coach is doing what he is doing.

Never scold your child in the presence of the team either at a practice or a game for what you feel he did or did not do.

Never insist that your child should play if he is ill or suffering from an injury. No child should be requested to play if he is in pain. It could result in long term injury which we all wish to avoid.

During a game, never shout and demean another team and its players by completely forgetting that the other team is made of children the same as your own.

During a game, don't take the officials to task over a call or calls that he has made. It will not change the officials decision and only reflects upon your team and your child.

A parent has the right;
To share in their child's training experience.
To encourage their child and the team.
To be concerned about their child's safety.
To see their child treated fairly.
To want their child's self esteem to grow.
To expect the coach to teach sportsmanship.
To expect the coach to set a good example.

A parent has the responsibility;

To get their child to practice on time.
To get their child to the game on time.
To notify the coach of illness.
To participate with team activities.

A parent has the responsibility for picking up their child after a practice or a game. If that is not possible, then advise the coach of who will be recovering the player so the coach will know.

Chapter 4

The Player Categories

Category I. Boys/Girls up through 2nd grade will use the intermediate youth basketball and the 8 1/2' basket. All players when on the court will wear sneakers. No hard soled shoes or cleats.

Coaching children in this category will revolve around the basic and elementary parts of basketball covered further in this book. This is the "how to" stage. Teaching the player how to dribble, move and dribble, how to put the ball up, how to pass to another player, and simple zone defense. Don't rush the "how to" phase, get the basics down as solid as you possibly can with the players.

It's important to let the children have fun. Please remember that youngsters in this category avoid, where possible, any physical aggression.

They want to play and not get hurt or to hurt anyone else. All of the children are competitive in their own way. Each child wants to be a good player and your encouragement will help them become that.

Young children are confused about aggressive behavior and think of it as hostility. Aggression is related to hostile acts, and as I tried to point out in the coaches section, you have no idea about your players outside environment. Don't consider the boxing out, close guarding or heavy shot blocking tactics with them. Instead show the guarding stances with arms raised which is intimidating enough. Help them to overcome their inherent shyness through team participation.

At least half of the training or practice session should be a light scrimmage so the players can be taught simple basketball rules. Instruct during the practice by stopping the game or scrimmage and explain about traveling, double dribble, hand checking, etc. Don't over do the instructions to the point the youngsters get intimidated. Loosen some of the rules so that they have fun at play.

Conditioning of children in this category should be limited to very light warm up exercises. These players have limited endurance and their activity is better directed at the training side of this program. Allow for their physical limitations and rest them as often as it seems necessary.

Category II. Boys/Girls in the 3/4 grade divisions will use the Women's Regulation size basketball and the standard height basket.

Coaching youngsters which fall into category II, should have them performing all of the elementary drills and part of the fundamental drills and exercises. Strategy and tactics are introduced in an elemental way to the fourth graders. These players possess most of the elementary skills and these skills can be built upon and polished.

At the expense of repeating myself, just in case you didn't read about Category I. Young children are confused about aggressive behavior and think of it as hostility. Aggression is related to hostile acts, and as I tried to point out in the coaches section, you have no idea about your players outside environment. Again move slowly when asking them to be physical against another player.

Teamwork is what must be emphasized at this level. The team must start working as a team. The majority of these players will continue to avoid any close personal physical contact. Aggressive play against another player in the physical sense just doesn't happen easily. Instead have them use their quickness and agility to get the ball around. Set up simple give and goes and perhaps teach some fast break philosophy.

Conditioning of these young players is a step above Category I in so far as their endurance is slightly better. They are by no means ready for the high activity seen with older players. To play a full game would be pushing the envelope a bit. If you overtire the players before practice or scrimmage begins, they will perform poorly, and that will have a negative effect on the players self image and their learning ability.

Use your warm up drills, practice drills, and then allow scrimmage to fill in the conditioning exercise you feel they must have. For one thing you have the players moving and getting their aerobics along with an improvement in endurance. Secondly they are having fun while getting into condition.

Category III. Boys in the 5th & 6th grades will use the Regulation size basketball and the standard height basket.

We are now talking about boys from age 10 or fifth grade to boys twelve in the 6th grade. This crossover age for the players is difficult. Puberty and all the pain of hormonal changes are taking place. Temperaments and mood swings greatly effect their ability to play and have fun. The very first priority is to create the team as a team. Get camaraderie building as quickly as possible. These players need the support of each other.

One minute you're coaching a child and the next minute a quasi young teenager. You must remain supportive and always talk to the entire team when you are coaching. First rule here again is to stress teamwork and good sportsmanship during play. Accept the tremendous differences between the 5th & 6th graders in age, size, aggression and ability.

To youngsters, aggression is related to hostile acts, and as I tried to point out in the coaches section, you have no idea about your players outside environment. Make aggressive rebounding, passing, cutting and ball handling hard, fast and quick. Let that be your view of aggressive playing. Don't encourage aggressive physical encounters against other players, that is not what aggressive play should be about.

Never condone nor instruct them in the use of excessive physical behavior such as shoving a boy from the back who has the ball. This is the time to begin with the in bounding routines, give and goes, boxing out drills, rebounding drills, defensive and offensive strategies and tactics. Some of it will stick, just a little, don't concern yourself about that too much. If they pick up one good habit a practice you may consider yourself a good coach.

At this juncture you must explain the value of the assist and what it means to the teams score. For instance a player gets six goals good for twelve points and four assists. Those four assists add another eight points to the teams score. Therefore the player can appreciate the value of the assists he has made when by his or her effort they have added twenty points overall.

Conditioning of these young players is a step above Category II in so far as their endurance is slightly better. They are by no means ready for the high activity seen with older players. They are marginal in endurance if a player is requested to play a full game. The normal physical condition of these children will vary widely the same as their maturity.

Use your warm up drills, practice drills, and then allow scrimmage to fill in the conditioning exercise you feel they must have. For one thing you have the players moving and getting their aerobics along with an improvement in endurance. Secondly they are having fun while getting into condition.

Category IV. Boys in the 7th through 8th grade will use the Regulation size basketball and the standard height basket.

Category IV covers the boys from 7th to 8th grades who are now teenagers. For the most part, these players have a lot of good skills and are ready to blossom under your leadership. Again the idea of teamwork must be stressed. Player and team disciplines will be the coaches primary concern. Strategies and tactics will be the main thrust in coaching both offense and defense.

Players at this age will begin to soak up strategies and tactics like a dry sponge. Improvements in playing techniques will begin to amaze you as a coach. Guarding, boxing out, going up for rebounds, following the ball in when it's put up. Setting picks and screens, fast breaks, give and goes, cuts, ball handling and passing.

I'm repeating myself but again explain the value of the assist and what it means to the teams score. When a player gets six goals good for twelve points and four assists. Those four assists add another eight points to the teams score. The player can appreciate the value of the assists when by his or her effort they have added twenty points overall.

These players are more physical than younger players, and comprehend the idea of aggressive play in order to take control of the ball and the court. Assertive play is without hostility and understood by youngsters of this age group. Competition has become fun. They love to win of course, but if they lose a game, it's not the end of the world.

Temper their aggressive playing with a thorough instruction about hand checking, shoving and excessive physical contact. Adolescents have temper outbursts which can quickly develop into hitting and fighting with their opponents. If during a practice or league game, one of your players becomes violent, bench'em. Never, I repeat, never allow one of your players to become a court bully. Good sportsmanship is what we are teaching, and what this game should be about.

Conditioning of these young athletes is a jump ahead of Categories I, II, & III. You are now dealing with players who have their hormones in place and their endurance has taken a quantum leap. Do your warm up drills in such a way as to break a sweat. Speed up their practices and ask them to hustle all of the time they are on court.

Work in wind sprints before scrimmage. During scrimmage, insist on hustle. No spectators, only participants are on court! Allow them their breaks and watch for tiring. If they run out of gas, stop the scrimmage and allow them to finish the last few minutes free balling. Conditioning is exercise, not an ordeal.

Chapter 5

Practice Schedule planning

It all begins with the amount of time allocated to the sports program by either the school, YMCA, Youth Foundation, Parks and Recreations Sport Office, Inner City Athletics, etc. Depending on the categories of your players, you may be given a game schedule from eight to twelve or more weeks.

This begins a string of questions you will have to deal with. What is the amount of time allowed for a practice session, and how many sessions may you have per week? How much practice will there be prior to your first game? Considering the age and ability of your team and its players, how much can you reasonably accomplish before your first game?

How do you start planning your practices? That is based upon the facilities available to you and their times of availability. It is also based upon the availability of your team members. It can't be during school hours, so it must be after school. Most of the basketball courts will be closed to practice on the weekends because that is normally when they will schedule games. However you do have a preseason period which may change some of those restrictions in your favor.

I suggest that you plan your practices right after school or during the early evening. Avoid late evening practices if possible. Schedule your court practice time on any day Monday through Friday. For some of you, there may be Sunday practices if facilities are available. If no indoor courts are available, consider outdoor courts at the parks or schools.

If you are coaching very young players, the earlier in the evening the better for them. There is also the consideration of when the parents are able to bring the kids to practice. In formulating the practice schedule you have to take into account all of the factors which comprise the team as a whole. That is the availability of yourself, the players and the parents along with the facility.

Use a practice scrimmage among your team players and attempt to assess their weakness' and their strengths. Based upon your observation you are now able to determine the type of instruction to be given. For the most part, your younger players will require the greatest amount of time in the basics.

When you prioritize the players needs in training, be realistic. Keep an honest perspective of what can and cannot be achieved with a limited amount of practice and training time. Refrain from having expectations that are beyond the abilities of the kids. Don't be intimidated by the game schedule. Set a steady learning pace for the team and let the win or loss of a game become secondary.

Make a chart. The left hand side or column represents your time frame. On the right side place the exercises or drills you want to have the players practice. Allow for your breaks and allow for scrimmages. As you progress with your training program, you will begin removing some of the earlier exercises and replacing them with new ones. Follow your plan. Obtain your teams training goals and their success.

As a general example, let's assume we can have a one hour practice session once or twice a week. How do you make something happen during such a short period of time? We start by breaking down the one hour into segments.

Allow the first five minutes to be free ball exercise with the players shooting and rebounding as they wish. Restrict the players from long ball shooting from mid court, otherwise anything goes. This is a way of setting the mood for practice.

Take the next thirty minutes to run the warm up and practice drills you feel they must do. Keep order on the court and critique their individual performance during those drills you have selected. You may be using the most basic drills or high order strategies and tactics, it all depends on the abilities and category of your team.

Take a five minute break and allow the team time for restrooms or drinking fountain use, and free ball play.

Use the twenty minutes for scrimmage to observe if the players are using what you instructed in drills. If not, blow the whistle and tell them what you want to see happening. Here is where you will be able to again demonstrate, instruct, coach and train the players in what you expect them to do. If an individual needs help, this is the time to give it.

In **Category I**, my experience has been that courts were available on Saturdays. You are allotted one hour of court time which breaks down into thirty minutes of training with a five minute break for restrooms and water fountain use. Following that, you have a practice or division game comprised of four, five minute quarters. The half time break of five minutes is again for restroom and water fountain use.

The regular basketball courts width is used as the court played on by children in this age group. The 8 1/2' baskets are in place with foul shot lanes defined. For kids in this category, that is plenty of room and about all that they can handle during running and play. Depending on how many teams are in your division, you may only be allowed to use one of the baskets while another team uses the other.

At this age level of youngsters, the referee will often blow the whistle for a time out to give instructions to the youngsters on rules of the game. This is as it should be. What we are doing is teaching the very basics of the game and allowing the children to have fun. I would also recommend that you have a booster session at games end, pointing out the many good things that the children were able to do.

An example of a practice session for beginners.

First five minutes allow the youngsters to have free play.

Next 25 minutes:

Do stretching, twisting and squat exercises

Start warm ups using the guarding stance and lateral movements.

Work on dribbling drills across the court.

Work on passing drills: Bounce and Chest.

Begin shooting drills close in to the backboard.

Do both lateral side and free throw shots.

Five Minute Break for water and restroom use, with free play.

Final Period of Practice.

Split the team into two equal numbers for team play.

Show positions for defense and offense.

Conduct your scrimmage adding instructions for team play which will re-enforce the earlier training portion.

All of this is in keeping with T-Ball for youngsters who play baseball. It is almost always a Saturday game with time allotments. Saturdays are for the little people. The difference in T-Ball and basketball is the facilities and their availability for practice. A court is much more difficult to find than the school yard diamond.

If you can locate accommodations for court practice, break it down to the most basic fundamentals of the game. This is the "how to" stage of training. Limit your practice time to one hour. Give rest breaks often. As your team progresses, slowly schedule into the practice your elementary drills. Begin your program with the "how to" routines and then move to the elementary drills. Make a chart of time and drills and put them into use the first session you have.

In the **Category II** which is third and fourth grade, schedule in a one hour practice session per week. Normally these youngsters will be scheduled for their games on a Saturday. Categories III and IV are more often than not, played during the week in the evenings. The games scheduled for evening play can become a problem for scheduling your practice sessions. The best hours for children in this group is before seven p.m.

The regular basketball courts width is used as the court practiced on by children in this age group. The regulation height baskets are in place with foul shot lanes defined. For kids in this category, that is plenty of room for practice and scrimmage. Depending on how many teams are in your division, you may only be allowed to use one of the baskets while another team uses the other.

An example of a practice session

First five minutes allow the youngsters to have free play.

Next 25 minutes:

Do warm up drills for 5 minutes.

Finish warm up drill with guarding stance and lateral movement.

Practice pivots both right and left side.

Do two man running and passing drill across court width.

Begin with running lay ups, 3 rotations each side.

Work on passing drills at the key. Bounce and Chest.

Offensive rebounding using feint and step past defense.

Fakes & Pivots.

Simple stutter step offensive move past defender with ball.

Fake and pivot to move ball in a break away.

Player assignments & positions

At basket, defense positions and coverage.

At basket, offensive positions and movements.

Five Minute Break for water and restroom use, with free play.

Final Period of Practice.

Split the team into two equal numbers for team play.

Show positions for defense and offense.

Conduct your scrimmage adding instructions for team play which will re-enforce the earlier training portion.

Scrimmage for these players is still a practice. Make certain they can understand what you have intended the scrimmage to be. Let them know what you are looking for from the practice you have just finished. It will work best if you use the whistle, stop the practice and walk them through what was just taught.

Children in the category should be able to perform all of the basic and elementary drills we have defined. They are also capable of doing simple give and goes, offense and defense positions, out-of-bounds box plays, and running passing routines.

If you are scheduled for a Saturday game, arrange your practice on either Wednesday, Thursday or Friday. I shouldn't have to tell you that, but I going to anyway and the reasons are obvious. More of the practice session will be retained and used by the players than if they have had a longer layoff. The fresher the practice session, the better the game. The better they play, the better they feel and the better job you are doing.

Category III is a whole new ball game for these kids. I suggest that you schedule at least two practice sessions a week regardless of the games played. You will have practice and league games which will be split between Saturdays and week nights. The practice session should be one hour, no more, no less.

These players are capable of performing all basic, elementary and a good part of the fundamental practices and drills. Your guide lines will be more detailed and directed than in the previous practice session. You will also be introducing elementary strategies and tactics and perhaps a set play or two.

It is a must that they learn in-bounding play patterns for under the basket and along the sidelines. It is a must that they learn the half court press and full court press patterns. It is a must for them to know how to play man-to-man and modified zone defense. Boxing out, rebounding and fast breaks should be done during scrimmages. This category of players is the crossover time for the youngsters. They are going from children to adolescents.

What is taught here, especially to the sixth grade players will be their foundation for the next year. Start early with these players and have them know their areas of responsibility when playing a given position.

An example of a practice session
First five minutes Warm up drills stressing guarding movements.
Next 25 minutes:
Lay-up drill: 3 rotations on right side, switch lines and do three rotations from the left side.
High Post Give and Goes:
    3 rotations on the right side, switch lines
    3 rotations on the left side.
Forwards Practice:
    Shooting their zone-pass-no bounce & put it up.
    Use mid/low post "X" pass pattern with put it up and player rotation. Rebounding must be on the jump.
    Feint, pivot and put it up.
    Feint, pivot, break and pass across (bounce or chest).
    Feint, pivot and pass, receiver puts it up.
Guards Practice:
    High post give and goes from left & right sides
    High post break away and pass.
    High post feint, pivot and put it up with a jump.
    High post pivot, break to basket and put it up.
All Team:
    Outside pass around & move around-no put ups.
    Run-Stop and shoot over a screen.
    Emphasize position areas and circulation on offense.
Five Minute Break for water and restroom use, with free play.
Final Period of Practice.
Split the team into two equal numbers for team play. Work on 2-3 defense and 2-3 offensive positions. Use call out on fast break to alert other team members that they have ball possession.

Category IV is a new step up for everyone involved. This is where hustle begins and just playing ends. I suggest that you schedule at least two practice sessions a week regardless of the games played. You will have practice and league games which will be split between Saturdays and week nights. The practice session should be no less than one hour and a little more if possible.

<h2 style="text-align:center">An example of a practice session</h2>

First five minutes Warm up drills stressing guarding movements.

Next 25 minutes:

Lay-up drill: 3 rotations on right side, switch lines and do three rotations from the left side.

High Post Give and Goes:

> 3 rotations on the right side, switch lines
> 3 rotations on the left side.

All Team:

> Outside pass around & move around-no put ups.
> Run-Stop and shoot over a screen.
> Emphasize position areas and circulation on offense.
> Work on communications during play.
> Work on fast break strategy and outlet man.
> Work on pick and roll from top of key and mid post
> Do 1-3-1 rotation formation and practice all players in both offense and defense.
> Work all in-bounding routines from side line and under the basket positions. Let each player play each position.
> Work rebounding exercise.
> Work both jump and fade-away shots.

Guards Practice:

> Long ball put ups & overhead passing to Forwards.

Forwards Practice: Hook and Backboard.

Five Minute Break for water and restroom use, with free play.

Final Period of Practice.

Split the team into two equal numbers for team play. Work on 2-3 defense and 2-3 offensive positions. Use call out on fast break to alert other team members that they have ball possession. Encourage lots of hustle on the court at all times.

We have finally reached the arena of strategies and tactics. Set plays can now be introduced and practiced to perfection. That is if all of the basics are in place. Evaluate the team capabilities as quickly as possible then start to build on their strengths. Some would say, no, no, you begin by overcoming their weakness'. I consider that a negative approach to building the teams potential.

Players in this age group have a strong tendency to emulate the other players on the team who are better players and learn from them. They quickly pick up from each other, so that you don't have to concentrate on the basics as you must with the younger players. They are also more interested in helping each other become better. As a result, your better players will always help the less skilled players to improve without you making a point of it.

Speed, hustle, teamwork, hustle, shot polishing, and hustle is what you strive for during practice and game play. Fundamentals in guarding, rebounding, boxing out offense, boxing out defense must all be done with aggressive quickness. Now is the time when you must get your players feet off of the floor. Get them to fly like eagles. Go up with the ball when shooting. Work hard on jump shots. Go up when they pass over defense.

Practice Facilities

The facilities you will use are based upon the locations available to you. If you are lucky enough to get courts which belong to your local Parks and Recreation Department they will look something like the court layout like the following. A court with baskets set at court width allows the Category

I a complete playing court and all other categories great training and scrimmage courts.

This is also true for your local YMCA courts which have excellent training facilities for young players. There are some middle school courts and junior high school courts which take on this configuration.

You may not have courts this nice available to your program. If you only have outdoor courts in the park or on a school ground, you will have to become very creative with games for Category I. The other categories will play half court practice and scrimmages. Taking this into consideration, all of the illustrations for exercise and drills are based on a half court plan.

So what I've done is to lay out the drills and practices on a regulation half court without baskets at width. However you will notice that I ask that if you have more than one basket, put them all into use.

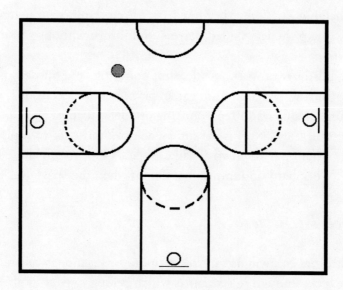

Chapter 6

Fundamental Elements
of the Game

1. Dribbling the basketball.

Category I. Young players with small hands may use the entire hand for bouncing the ball in the vertical plane. The height of the bounce should not be much above the players waist and may require extended arm pump to keep the ball in a rhythmic motion. Begin the exercise with the player using the hand he normally uses for other exercises.

If right handed use the right hand, if left handed use the left hand. He may remain in one spot until he develops enough skill to begin walking forward with the ball while maintaining the bouncing rhythm. Avoid carrying the ball by placing the palm under the ball and rotating over the ball as the ball is being bounced. That is a traveling foul.

Most of these youngsters will have a tendency to dribble directly in front of themselves where they can easily watch the ball and control it. You need not be overly concerned about having them dribble to one side or the other of the body. It is difficult enough for the beginner to keep the ball in motion.

Category II, III & IV. Will use the fingers, thumb and finger bridge only-no palm or heel of hand to touch the ball while bouncing the ball in the vertical plane. The height of the bounce should not be above the players waist and require only forearm pump to keep the ball in a rhythmic motion. Begin the exercise with the player using the hand he normally uses for other exercises.

If right handed use the right hand, if left handed use the left hand. He may remain in one spot until he develops enough skill to begin walking forward with the ball while maintaining the bouncing rhythm. Finger and hand flex gives the dribbler the greatest amount of ball and bounce control. Avoid carrying the ball by placing the palm under the ball and rotating over the ball as the ball is being bounced. That is a traveling foul.

Let your players know that the shorter the distance the ball has to travel from the hand, the more control they have. If the body is lowered during a dribble, the time between release of the ball and its rebound back into the hand is greatly shortened. The tactile feel of the ball in the hand is almost constant. This allows the player to rotate his hand over the ball and give its bounce direction with spin.

2. Ball Passing:

Passing drills and proper passing techniques are of the most fundamental importance. Passing is done from the stationary position, on the run, and from the jump. Poor technique and lack luster passing can ruin a teams chances of winning play. This is where the majority of turn overs come from. The player who loses the ball giving a soft or lob pass is the one who is at fault. It requires the very best of skills and concentration from the player.

The first order of business is for them to look where they are passing. Make eye contact with their intended receiver. The eye contact tells the intended passer that the receiver knows where the ball is, and can expect to receive it.

Chest & Bounce Passing

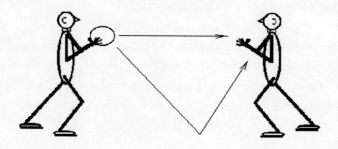

The ball, with few exceptions, is passed using both hands. The ball must be under control by the passer before he ever attempts the release. Passing requires as much skill as shooting for a basket in a game. When running and passing, the passer must judge where the receiver is going to be when the ball gets to him. How much distance does he lead the receiver by? It will take a lot of practice to learn that simple rule. The passes by and large are as follows:

Bounce passing-bounce the ball towards the receiver with the ball contacting the court two thirds of the distance from the passer.

Chest high passing-Passing at chest level to the receiver.

Overhead pass-passing with the arms overhead, flexing the wrists toward the receiver.

Side passes-passing from a swiveled positions, either chest or bounce to receiver.

Baseball-or long pass from back-court towards mid-court and used in fast break situation. It is almost thrown like a football.

Reach around pass against a defender can be either single or double handed and from the position of facing the defender or with your back to him.

Hook pass overhead-like a hook shot, it's made with the hand away from the defender and directed into the receiver.

Passing behind the back-is not recommended for young players due to too many turn-overs and sometimes injuries.

3. Shooting Techniques.

Putting the ball up is what the game boils down to. Dribbling and passing is the method of play used to get the player in position to shoot. And the variation on the theme of how the ball goes up is almost endless. When you are coaching this "how to" shoot, I suggest that you don't rush it. Youngsters put a lot of pressure on themselves to excel in the game, and shooting is what they consider the main part of the game to be.

When the shooter is standing close to the basket at an angle, have him use the backboard. It improves the chances of making the basket by fifty percent. Close up and close in angle shots are considered soft shots and they are made with "touch". By that I mean just above the rim with a controlled light effort. Lay-ups are the "ready cash" shots of the game. When your kids begin making baskets, it is a real confidence builder.

Currently the most popular way to put up the ball is using the one hand shot. That involves the arm in a shoving motion and the hand and wrist with a shove/flex motion. At the beginning, the player should be positioned close to the basket, with the shoulders squared facing the backboard.

Let's assume the player is right handed. The left hand is placed under the ball for lifting assistance and to steady the sphere. The right hand is placed over the ball, with the finger tips spread along one the longitudinal seams. This aids in gripping and holding the ball until release. This should become a normal habit in time, but in the beginning, it sets your start point.

Once the shoulders are squared to the basket, move the right foot slightly forward. This aligns the foot, ankle, hip and arm in the direction the ball will travel. Now, take a slight squatting stance, then shove upward from the right foot as the hand, arm and upper body extends upward towards the basket. The ball is propelled with a forward snap at the hand and wrist.

The release of the ball should move upwards in an arc to the goal. The player is looking at the basket, and can see the ball moving in the direction it is catapulted. Therefore he is able to see the ball from initiation into flight.

The two handed shooter does not spread his finger on the seams. Instead the ball is grasped on the opposite ends. His shoulders and feet are squared to the basket, and the ball is put up moving from the chest upwards as he rises from the slight squat.

The hook shot is a more difficult play to make because it is almost a put it up by feel. It is used for making a basket and as a pass over defense. It requires the player to align his shoulders in the direction he will pass. Therefore if right handed, the left shoulder points towards the basket and the right shoulder aligns with it on a line to the basket. The right hand, with arm extended loops the ball up and over the head and shoulder. The ball is released towards the basket, the angle varies with the distance from the basket. This shot is usually made from within or near the key.

Let's look at how the feet are placed during shooting to align the body with the basket. In a stationary position they will look like the following for right handed shooting, two handed chest shots and left handed shooter. What we are doing here is aligning the foot, ankle, arm, elbow and hand towards the basket.

Keep this in mind when practicing foul shots, and stationary shots in front of the basket. If right handed, the right foot is placed in line with the basket at the center of the key. That holds true for the left handed shooter, it's his left foot in line with the basket at the center of the key. The two handed shooter squares up and gets to center his body.

Right Handed Shooter   Two Handed Shooter

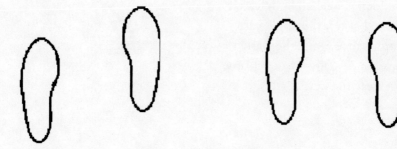

Left Handed Shooter

Chapter 7

Warm Up Drills

The warm up drills are intended to exercise the body in such a way as to compliment the practice drills. Muscles and ligaments used during play should be stretched and warmed before active drills are run. What we are interested in here is the ham string, Achilles tendon, lower back and upper shoulders.

Those drills listed below are only a few of the many possibilities now available to you. Employ as many other or different ones as you are familiar with, and use them judiciously. Categories I & II require the most gentle exercises. Beyond those categories expand freely, but do not turn an exercise into an ordeal.

Waist, Torso & Upper Body-Warm-up No. 1.

Form the players into two lines that face you from left to right and two players deep. Have them spread out sideways until their fingers cannot touch.

Have them spread their feet shoulder width facing you. On the first count with hands on hips, have them twist their torso to face their upper bodies to the left. Second count returns them to facing you, the third count have them twist their torso to face their upper bodies to the right. Fourth count returns them to facing forward again. Do twelve cycles.

Waist, Torso & Upper Body-Warm-up No. 2.

Form the players into two lines that face you from left to right and two players deep. Have them spread out sideways until their fingers cannot touch.

Have them spread their feet shoulder width facing you. On the first count with arms extended at shoulder height sideways , have them twist their torso to face their upper bodies to the left.

Second count returns them to facing you, the third count have them twist their torso to face their upper bodies to the right. Fourth count returns them to facing forward again. Do twelve cycles.

Waist, Torso & Upper Body-Warm-up No. 3.

Form the players into two lines that face you from left to right and two players deep. Have them spread out sideways until their fingers cannot touch. Have them spread their feet shoulder width facing you. On the first count with hands on their hips, have them bend forward and reach for their toes.

Second count returns them upright to facing you, on the third count have them bend their upper bodies backwards. Fourth count returns them to upright facing forward again. Do twelve cycles.

Vertical Body Stretch and Calf-Warm-up No. 4.

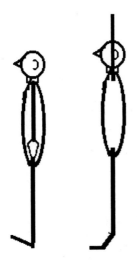

Form the players into two lines that face you from left to right and two players deep. Have them spread out sideways until their fingers cannot touch. Have them spread their feet slightly apart and hands at their sides facing you.

On the first count rock backwards on the heels while lifting the toes from the floor. Second count rocks them forward onto their toes and up as they raise their hands and arms reaching for the ceiling. The third count returns them to their starting position. Do twelve cycles.

Vertical Body Stretch and Side-Warm-up No. 5.

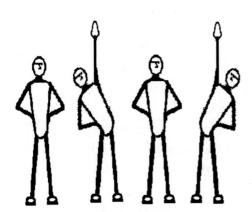

Form the players into two lines that face you from left to right and two players deep. Have them spread out sideways until their fingers cannot touch. Have them spread their feet shoulder width and hands on their hips facing you.

On the first count raise their left hand reaching for the

ceiling and bending to their right side. Second count returns them to the start position. Third count raise their right hand reaching for the ceiling and bending to their left side. Fourth count returns them to the start position. Do twelve cycles.

Leg Lunge and Quadriceps-Warm-up No. 6.

At one end of the court, form the players into three lines. Each line will follow the person at the head of the line. With their back straight, step forward with the right foot, plant the foot and lower the body until the left knee touches the floor. Hold a moment then push back to the up position and pull the left foot even with the right.

With their back straight, step forward with the left foot, plant the foot and lower the body until the right knee touches the floor. Hold a moment then push back to the up position and pull the right foot even with the left.

Continue the exercise until the players have crossed the width of the court. This is not a hurry up exercise, take your time. Some of the small players may have difficulty, if so, shorten the length of the training path.

Leg Squats and Quadriceps-Warm-up No. 7.

Form the players into two lines that face you from left to right and two players deep. Have them spread out sideways until their fingers cannot touch. Have them spread their feet shoulder width and hands on their hips facing you. On the first count have them squat with arms forward, outstretched for balance until the legs are folded. Second count returns them to their original position. Do twelve cycles.

Side Straddle Hop-Warm-up No. 8.

Form the players into two lines that face you from left to right and two players deep. Have them spread out sideways until their fingers cannot touch. Have them place their feet together and hands at their sides facing you. On the count of one, they must jump vertically, spreading their feet and raising their hands overhead to clap. On the second count they return to their starting position. You may use a two count or four count cadence.

Court Sprint-Warm-up No. 9.

At one end of the court, form the players into three lines. The first player in each line will sprint forward until mid court line and touch the line marking. On the return sprint they will go to the back of their own starting line.

When the first player returns, the second player repeats what the first player has done, until all players have completed the pattern. Add interest by having the lines compete to finished first.

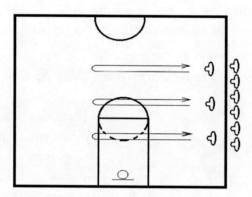

Court Circuit Jogging-Warm-up No. 10.

This is not a race. Slow jog the perimeter of the court, shaking out the arms and hands. This is intended to be a loosening up jog. Get the blood flowing and the entire body warmed up. The number of circuits will depend on the children's ages and conditions. Don't make it an ordeal, it's just a simple warm-up that you can start or finish with.

Vertical Jump-Warm-up No. 11.

Form the players into two lines that face you from left to right and two players deep. Have them spread out sideways until their fingers cannot touch. What we want is to have the players jump as high with arms going up on the jump as they can reach. The cadence is jump, bounce,

bounce, jump, bounce, bounce. The bounce is a short vertical jump above ankle high.

The intention of the drill is to teach the players how to go up for a rebound, defensive pass blocking, over defense shooting and passing. It is primarily for the older players who must learn to fly and get above the defense during game play.

Chapter 8

Practices & Drills

"HOW TO" Dribbling Practices:
Change hands while dribbling.

The Exercise:

Have the players remain in one spot while practicing the dribble. The player will bounce the ball at a spot in front of himself and toward the side of the hand he is dribbling with. As an example, he/she will bounce the ball in front of and to the right of the right foot if the dribbler is right handed.

Bounce a ten count with the hand of choice, then have the player bounce the ball to a spot in front of his/her feet and pick up the bounce count with the other hand. Using the ten count, practice the exercise through five change overs.

Moving forward while dribbling.

The Exercise:

Having established that the player understands the basics of dribbling, have them move across the width of the court and return while dribbling with one hand. The basic young beginners may walk, but at a jog is preferable. Repeat this drill until each player can at least slow jog the exercise.

The next step is to have the player repeat the drill using the opposite hand for dribbling. Repeat this drill until each player can at least slow jog the exercise.

Dribble with either hand while moving forwards.

The Exercise:

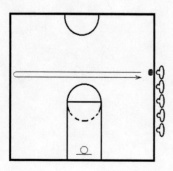

Have the players start with their hand of choice, and at a jogging gate, dribble the width of the court. At the halfway point in crossing, have the player switch the ball to the opposite hand and continue until reaching the end point. Do the same on the return crossing to their starting point.

Dribbling Drill:

Set up two or more equal groups of players on one side of the court. Have them compete in a race crossing and returning to their point of origin. When the player returns, he/she passes the ball to the next player in line. The first group to complete the circuit with all players is declared the winning team.

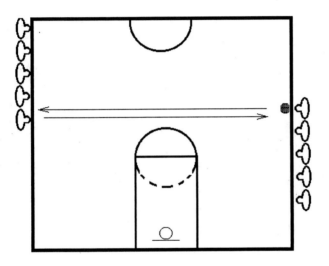

Select each of the previous dribbling techniques listed and run the competition drill. Stress using peripheral vision to see the ball without watching the balls bounce. Keep the ball low when dribbling.

"HOW TO" Passing Practices:

In all passing practices, the passer moves towards the receiver. By doing so the passer gets extra momentum on the ball and improves his/her accuracy. Like shooting, the motion squares the shoulders in the two handed pass. The intended receiver should move forward to receive the pass.

Chest & Bounce Passing

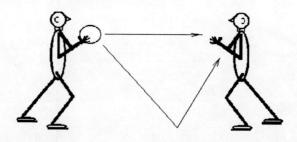

The Bounce Pass

Divide your team into two equal number of players and align them along the outside lane markers of the key, facing each other. This is a distance of twelve feet and the best place to start your youngest players to practice. Older players may align the same way with each side taking one or more steps backwards to open the distance. Each player on one side will be given a basketball to pass to their opposing team member who will become the receivers.

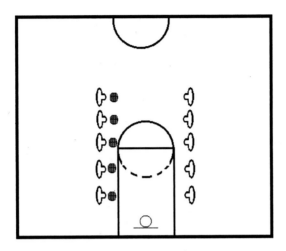

From the chest level position of the ball, have the passers step forward and pass it across the key. The ball should bounce 2/3 rds of the distance across with the receiver stepping forward to catch it. Now the receiver becomes the passer and repeats the process. What you are looking for here is accuracy and reasonable ball speed.

The Chest High Pass

Divide your team into two equal number of players and align them along the outside lane markers of the key, facing each other. This is a distance of twelve feet and the best place to start your youngest players to practice. Older players may align the same way with each side taking one or more steps backwards to open the distance. Each player on one side will be given a basketball to work with, their opposing team players will become the receivers.

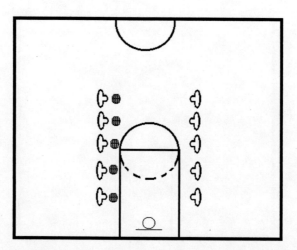

From the chest level position of the ball, have the passers step forward and pass it across the key. The receiver should step forward to catch the ball at chest level. Now the receiver becomes the passer and repeats the process. What you are looking for here is accuracy and reasonable ball speed.

The Overhead Pass

Divide your team into two equal number of players and align them along the outside lane markers of the key, facing each other. This is a distance of twelve feet and the best place to start your youngest players to practice. Older players may align the same way with each side taking one or more steps backwards to open the distance. Each player on one side will be given a basketball to pass with, their opposing team players will become the receivers.

The passer will pass with the arms overhead, flexing the wrists toward the receiver sending the ball forward. The receiver should step forward to catch the ball at chest level or above. Now the receiver becomes the passer and repeats the process. What you are looking for here is accuracy and reasonable ball speed.

The Overhead Hook Pass

Divide your team into two equal number of players and align them along the outside lane markers of the key, facing each other. This is a distance of twelve feet and the best place to start your youngest players to practice. Older players may align the same way with each side taking one or more steps backwards to open the distance. Each player on one side will be given a basketball to work with, their opposing team players will become the receivers.

This is like a hook shot, it's made with the hand away from the defender and directed into the receiver. The passer turns sideways to the receiver, and align his shoulders with the receiver. The hand holding the ball is away from the receiver. Like a hook shot, the passer must sweep the ball up and over his head and release it in such a way as to be caught by the receiver.

The receiver should step forward to catch the ball at chest level or above. Now the receiver becomes the passer and repeats the process. What you are looking for here is accuracy and reasonable ball speed.

The Side Pass

Form the team into a circle with approximately six feet between the players. Have them face outwards, not inwards. Use two balls, one on each opposing side of the circle. On your start signal, have the balls passed to the left. Each player should keep his feet planted and twist to the side to either receive or pass the ball. After several rounds have been completed, have the players reverse the direction of the ball. Make several circuits and allow the players to understand how passing can be done without a pivot.

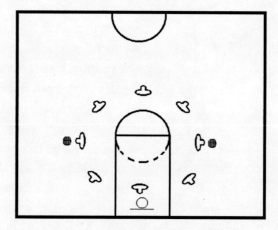

With the players still in a circle, have them face inwards where all of the players can see each other. Use two balls, one on each opposing side of the circle. On your start signal, have the balls passed to the left. Each player should keep his feet planted and twist to the side to either receive or pass the ball.

After several rounds have been completed, have the players reverse the direction of the ball. Have the passing speed up to see if one ball can catch up to the other.

The Baseball Pass.

For the baseball pass, split your players into passers & receivers. Passers on one side of the courts width and receivers on the other side. Have the passers throw the basketball across the courts width to the receiver. A bounce is quite acceptable if not preferred.

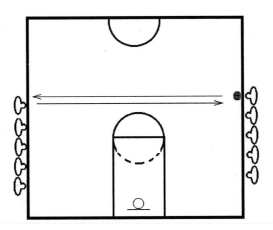

The receiver then becomes the passer and returns the ball with a baseball pass. In a physical sense, the throw is more like a football pass than a baseball throw. This type of pass becomes effective during a fast break situation, or during a difficult full court press against the inbounding team.

Smaller children may have to use both hands to push-pass the ball as far as they can, older players will have more ability to throw the ball.

The Reach Around Pass.

Reach around pass is used against defense to get the ball to a player who is cutting to the basket or an open spot. It usually happens when you are trapped. Break your players into groups of three as shown in the diagram.

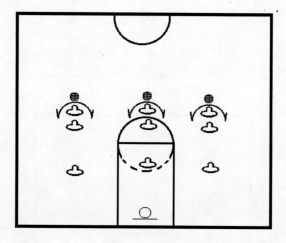

The front player with the ball will practice reaching with a twist to pass to the man farthest behind. The passer may pivot slightly if necessary. Have the players pass from both left and right sides.

The passer them moves to the rear of that line, the defender becomes the passer and the receiver becomes the defender. Do not pressure the passer, this is a twist and pass practice.

At The Key Passing.

Form a box of four players, you may use the corners of the key. This is high post to low post. low post to low post, low post to high post, high post to high post. This is running counter clockwise around the lane. After four complete circuits, reverse the passing to clockwise.

Alternate the passing technique with chest pass, bounce pass, overhead pass and hook pass.

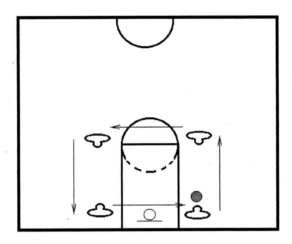

Using the same box pattern with the players, switch the passing pattern to a figure eight. That requires the ball to travel diagonally across the box. Alternate the passing technique with chest pass, bounce pass, overhead pass and hook pass.

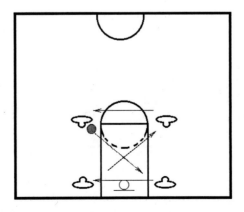

"HOW TO" Shooting Practices:
Elementary Shooting Drills for the beginning player.

The player will stand three feet back from the basket rim, facing the backboard. From this point have the player try to put the ball through the basket. Give him assistance on how to look at the rim and aim the ball upward. You may have to have him exaggerate his push off in order to get the ball high enough to reach the hoop. Stress the effect of good body balance in putting the ball up. Make sure that every player is in balance when they prepare to shoot.

Elementary Shooting Drill Exercise:

Place two players at forty-five degree angles in front of the basket at low post. Have player one put the ball up and player two rebound or recover the ball. Player number two now puts the ball up and player number one rebounds the shot. Both players now go to the end of their lines, and the next players in line step forward and repeat the drill.

When a moderate degree of success is reached, move the players back another three feet, and repeat the drill. At this point, show them how to use the backboard for close in shots. You are laying the foundation for running lay-ups.

Elementary Free throw or foul shots & Drill.

Have the shooter one third of the way in from the top of the key. Show him how to align his body and feet towards the goal. Make sure he or she has the leading foot slightly forward. Allow him to bounce the ball several times, then put it up.

Make it or not, have the shooter follow the ball in and get his own rebound, and pass it to the next player in line and return to the back of the practice line. If you have a player or players who are unable to shoot it to the basket, move them in closer.

Work from this location until some degree of proficiency is established. Encourage each effort. Don't allow the youngster to feel that he "just can't do it". All players must be given this practice. If your court has several backboards, put them all into use. This is hardest for the young players who are using the 8 1/2 foot high basket. Also the change to the regulation height.

Running Passes:
Elementary Category I running pass to intended receiver.

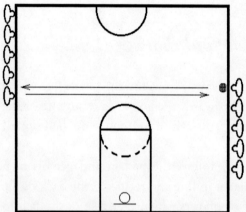

Divide your team into two equal number of players and place half on each side of the courts width. Give a basketball to one of the players at the head of the line. The player on "go" dribbles on the run towards the opposite side.

At the approach, the player bounce passes the ball forward to the receiver. The receiver now becomes the passer and dribbles on the run back across court to the next player in the other line who will become the receiver. Alternate bounce and chest passes during this drill.

Two man parallel running, passing with dribble

This drill will be across the width of the court. We begin with two players spread out approximately 10 to 12 feet. They will start from the line at the same time dribbling and jogging towards the far side. The player with the ball now bounce passes to the man running across from him. They continue passing back and forth as they run.

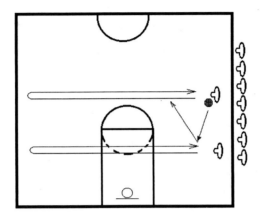

This exchange continues back and forth between the players until they reach the far side, where they will turn around and repeat the drill until they return to their starting point. The ball is passed to the next players in line who repeat the exercise. This exercise will use only the chest and bounce pass and both should be worked into the drill.

Two man parallel running, passing without dribble.

This drill will be across the width of the court. We begin with two players spread out approximately 10 to 12 feet. They will start from the line at the same time jogging towards the far side. One player will start with the ball. The player with the ball now bounce passes to the man running across from him. The player in possession of the ball must not dribble but return the pass to the first man while taking two running steps. The routine is quick receive, quick release.

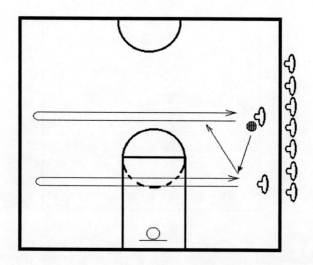

This exchange continues back and forth between the players until they reach the far side, where they will turn around and repeat the drill until they return to their starting point. The ball is passed to the next players in line who repeat the exercise. This exercise will use only the chest and bounce pass and both should be worked into the drill.

Three man parallel running, passing without dribble.

This drill will be across the width of the court. We begin with three players spread out approximately 10 to 12 feet apart. They will start from the line at the same time jogging towards the far side. The player in the center will start with the ball.

The player with the ball now bounce passes to the man running across from him to his right. The player in possession of the ball must not dribble but return the pass to the center man while taking two running steps. The center man now passes to the man on his left who receives the ball and returns it to the center man. The routine is quick receive, quick release.

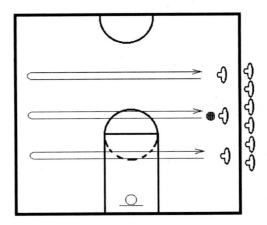

Here's how it goes, middle to right, right to middle, middle to left, left to middle, middle to right, etc. This drill supports the fast break type of passing, and aggressive offensive charging with a 2-3 offense formation.

This exchange continues back and forth between the players until they reach the far side, where they will turn around and repeat the drill until they return to their starting point. The ball is passed to the next players in line who repeat the exercise. This exercise will use only the chest and bounce pass and both should be worked into the drill.

Two man weave with lateral passes during crossovers.

This drill will be across the width of the court. Both players, the passer and receiver start together. One player will start with the ball, and dribble on the run. The players will run a crisscross pattern bounce passing to each other as they pass in the pattern.

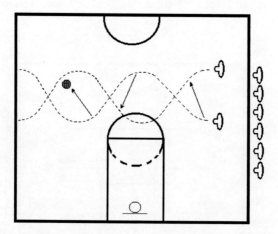

This exchange continues back and forth between the players until they reach the far side, where they will turn around and repeat the drill until they return to their starting point. The ball is passed to the next players in line who repeat the exercise. This exercise will use only the chest and bounce pass and both should be worked into the drill.

Three man Weave with lateral passes during crossovers.

This drill will be across the width of the court. Select your first three players and station them 7 to 8 feet apart. All players start together. The middle player will start with the ball, and dribble on the run. The players will run a crisscross pattern bounce passing to each other as they pass in the pattern.

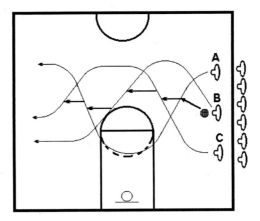

This exchange continues back and forth between the players until they reach the far side, where they will turn around and repeat the drill until they return to their starting point. The ball is passed to the next players in line who repeat the exercise. This exercise will use only the chest and bounce pass and both should be worked into the drill.

Chapter 9

Fundamental Shooting Drills:

Do not allow your players to waste time shooting from half court during practice, since it is not a shot used during normal play. Learn to use the backboard during lay-ups and short jump shots.

Two step lay-up jump shot

Form two lines of players at forty-five degree angles approaching the basket and backboard. The first player in line on the right side is passed the ball. If he is right handed, have him take his first step forward on the right foot. He will push off from the court with his left foot putting the ball up. Have the player use the backboard to bounce the ball into the basket.

The player on the left side comes forward as the player on the right side begins his approach. He will rebound the ball and pass it to the next player in line, and the go to the rear of the shooting line. The player who shot goes to the back of the rebounding

line. Continue the rotation until you feel all players have had an adequate amount of practice.

Next step is to have the shooting start from the left side so each player
gets the feel for putting up the ball from either side of the basket. Critique
the efforts to show the players how the body aligns when the knee goes up
in the direction of the basket When approaching from the left side, have
them put the ball up with the left hand.

Running lay-up from lateral approach lines.

Form two lines of players at forty-five degree angles approaching the
basket and backboard. Start the lines even with the free throw line in the
key. The first player in line on the right side is passed the ball. Dribbling at
a run, have the player approach the basket, then from your chosen takeoff
point, go up with the ball, for a lay-up. Do like the pro's, use the backboard to enhance the chance of making the goal.

The player on the left side comes forward as the player on the right side begins his approach. He will rebound the ball and pass it to the next player in line, and the go to the rear of the shooting line. The player who shot goes to the back of the rebounding line. Continue the rotation until you feel all players have had an adequate amount of practice.

Next step is to have the shooting start from the left side so each player gets the feel for putting up the ball from either side of the basket. When approaching from the left side, have them put the ball up with the left hand.

Lateral lay-up with give & go.

Form two lines of players at forty-five degree angles approaching the basket and backboard. Start the lines even with or above the free throw line in the key. The first player in line on the right side is given the ball. The player on "go" steps forward and passes to the man on his left and cuts towards the basket. The man with the ball bounce passes to the first man who is running in for the lay-up.

The player on the left side comes forward as the player on the right side makes the lay-up. He will rebound the ball and pass it to the next player in line, and the go to the rear of the shooting line. The player who shot goes to the back of the rebounding line. Continue the rotation until you feel all players have had an adequate amount of practice.

Next step is to have the shooting start from the left side so each player gets the feel for putting up the ball from either side of the basket. When approaching from the left side, have them put the ball up with the left hand.

Running jump lay-up from straight on approach.

Form two lines of players, one at the free throw line in the top of the key and one at a forty-five degree angle approaching the basket and backboard. Start the lines even with the free throw line in the key. The first player in line at the top of the key is passed the ball. Dribbling at a run, have the player approach the basket, then from your chosen takeoff point, go up with the ball, for a lay-up. Do like the pro's, use the backboard to enhance the chance of making the goal.

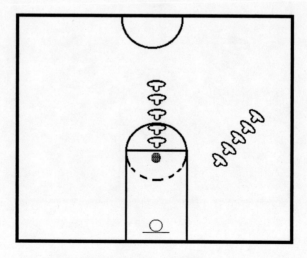

The player on the lateral side comes forward as the player from the key begins his approach. He will rebound the ball and pass it to the next player in line, and the go to the rear of the shooting line. The player who shot goes to the back of the rebounding line. Continue the rotation until you feel all players have had an adequate amount of practice.

Free-throw or foul shot at the top of the key.

Have the players line up at the top of the key. Show him how to align his body and feet towards the goal. Allow him to bounce the ball several times, then put it up. Make it or not, have the shooter follow the ball in and get his own rebound, and pass it to the next player and return to the back of the practice line. Encourage each effort. All players must be given this practice.

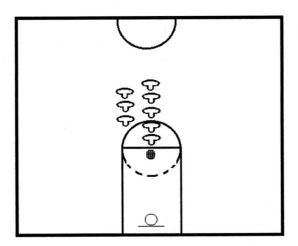

Most players will try to make it "all net", and that's fine. However do not overlook the use of the backboard. Also try to raise the arc in such as way as to be clearly over the rim. The raised arc puts the kinetic energy of the ball in a more downward direction, improving the chances of a goal. Rim skippers rebound like crazy and hardly ever go in.

If your court has several backboards, put them all into use. Divide your team into sub groups of equal number at each goal. On "go" have them compete in who can get to ten goals first. Another practice is to allow each boy or girl to shoot until they miss and declare a winner for each rotation.

Side line shots near three point line.

Divide your players into shooters and rebound's. Place these players on either side of the basket in alignment with the backboard. Have them one step inside of the backboard so they can see the goal clearly. From about twelve feet, have the shooters side take their shot, the ball will be rebounded by a rebounder from the opposite side and passed to the next player in line. The rebounder then joins the shooting line by going to the rear. The shooter joins the rebound's line at the rear.

Focus their attention on seeing the rim clearly, and on raising the arc of the ball to aid the percentage of goals. Repeat this exercise from the opposite side of the basket.

If your court has several backboards, put them all into use. Divide your team into sub groups of equal number at each goal. On "go" have them compete in who can get to ten goals first.

Hook shot against defense

The hook shot is primarily used to get the ball over a tough defender and into the net. It can be put up from any point in front of the backboard with reasonable success. The player puts the ball up with the hand away from the defender. It requires that the shoulders, arm and ball be aligned in the direction of the basket. The ball is tossed over the head with a sweeping arc motion, with the release almost overhead.

Usually the ball arc is not high and the backboard is bounced. It sounds difficult, but it isn't. Some players adapt to the shot quickly and it becomes an effective weapon for them during league play.

Use two players, one as shooter and one as defender. Station them in front of the hoop, and have the shooter put the ball up. Defender will rebound. Now have the players switch rolls. Work in groups of two until everyone has an opportunity to shoot.

If your court has several backboards, put them all into use. Divide your team into sub groups of equal number at each goal. Allow them time to develop a feel for the upward sweep.

Tap-In Shot Exercise & Drill.

When rebounding, the player should go up as high as he can, as the ball descends, he places his hand under it and shoves it back above the rim for a basket. Use the fingers to guide the ball when possible and do not overlook the backboard for help.

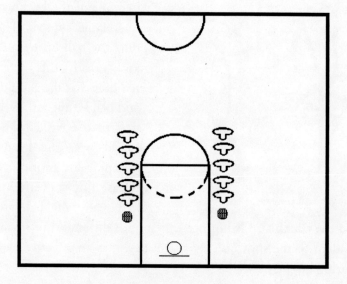

Break your team into two equal sections and have them form a line in front of the basket. The first player in each line stands half way to the foul shot line and to either side. The object is to put the ball up and have it bounce against the backboard. The right side line shoots to the right of the basket, the left side to the left of the basket.

At the ready signal, the first player in each line will move forward and put the ball up, following it in and going up for the Tap-In. The player then passes it to the next player in line and returns to the end of the line from which he came. Continue this rotation no less than five times, and until the movement becomes smooth.

At Key Passing and shooting.

Place your players on the outer edge of the key. Train them not to be in the key, for that is a penalty area when real play begins. Place the high post and low post players on right side of the key. Place the mid post player on the left side of the key. High post player will pass to low post using an overhead pass. Low post passes to mid post with an overhead pass. Mid post steps into the key and puts it up.

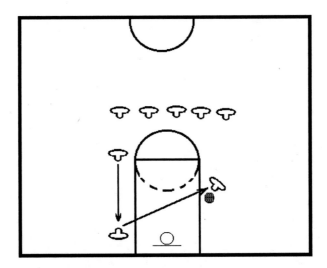

Now reverse and start with mid post to low post to high post who steps into the key and puts it up. Next it's high post to low post to mid post to low post, pivot and put it up. Repeat these three cycles using overhead, chest and bounce pass.

After five drill completion's, reverse the sides with high and low post on the left of the key and mid post to the right of the key. Repeat these three cycles using overhead, chest and bounce pass. As a final to this drill have the players rotate positions at the key.

Run-Stop-Jump shot. (straight on & lateral)

The run-stop practice is done to develop an offensive tactic when the player is under pressure from a defender running beside him to block the shot.

Form two lines of players at forty-five degree angles approaching the basket and backboard. Start the lines above the free throw line in the key. The first player in line on the right side is passed the ball. Dribbling at a run, have the player approach the basket, then SUDDENLY STOP, go up with the ball, for a jump shot. Do like the pro's, use the backboard to enhance the chance of making the goal.

The player on the left side comes forward as the player on the right side begins his approach. He will rebound the ball and pass it to the next player in line, and the go to the rear of the shooting line. The player who shot goes to the back of the rebounding line. Continue the rotation until you feel all players have had an adequate amount of practice.

Next step is to have the shooting start from the left side so each player gets the feel for putting up the ball from either side of the basket.

Run-Stop-Jump shot over a screen.

Form two lines of players at forty-five degree angles approaching the basket and backboard. Start the lines above the free throw line in the key. Set a player at mid post beside the lane facing the right side players line. This player now becomes the screen.

The first player in line on the right side is passed the ball. Dribbling at a run, have the player approach the screen, STOP, go up with the ball, for a jump shot over the screen. The screen should have his arms spread upward for blocking. Do like the pro's, use the backboard to enhance the chance of making the goal.

The player on the left side comes forward as the player on the right side begins his approach. He will rebound the ball and pass it to the next player in line, and the go to the screen position. The screen moves to the rear of the shooting line. The shooter goes to the back of the rebounding line.

Jump shots & Drill.

Have the player one third of the way in from the top of the key. Show him how to align his body and feet towards the goal. Have the player pump the ball one or more times, then spring straight upward with the shot. Make it or not, have the shooter follow the ball in and get his own rebound, and pass it to the next player in line and return to the back of the practice line.

Work from this location until some degree of proficiency is established. Continue moving the shooting position backwards until the shooter is at the free throw line. Guards should practice from 15 to 24 feet, forwards and centers should concentrate in the 12 to 20 feet.

"Fade Away" Jump shots & Drill.

Have the player one third of the way in from the top of the key. Show him how to align his body and feet towards the goal. Allow him to pump the ball one or more times, then spring upward and backwards with the shot. Make it or not, have the shooter follow the ball in and get his own rebound, and pass it to the next player in line and return to the back of the practice line.

Work from this location until some degree of proficiency is established. Continue moving the shooting position backwards until the shooter is at the free throw line. Guards should practice from 15 to 24 feet, forwards and centers should concentrate in the 12 to 20 feet.

Practice all shots from a jump-get it over the defense.

Find your best shooting range from the basket and polish it.

Chapter 10

Pivots & Feints for Offense:

A pivot by definition takes place when a player who is holding the ball steps once or more times in any direction with the same foot, while other foot is kept in contact with the floor. This allows the player to rotate in either direction away from an aggressive defender.

A fake or feint is a motion to create misdirection of the players intentions. There are numerous ways to employ the fake, such as the simple stutter step motion to get past a defender.

Elementary pivot practice

Have the players form two lines facing you. Have them separate until their outstretched arms can touch only at the finger tips. With the left foot planted as the pivot foot, have them rotate away from you and then rotate back towards you. Allow them to make a complete circle with the pivot foot remaining in place.

Now with the right foot planted as the pivot foot, have them rotate away from you and then rotate back towards you. Allow them to make a complete circle with the pivot foot remaining in place.

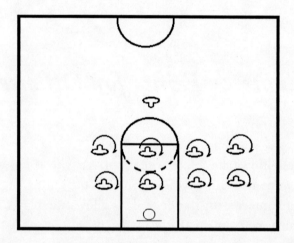

As the coach/trainer demonstrate these basic moves so that the young players know what you expect of them. Exaggerate your pivoting in order for them to get a clear picture of this important drill.

Fundamental pivot practice.

Break your players into groups of two. One player will have the ball and the other shall act as a defender. The defenders job will be to try and take the ball. The player with the ball will attempt to pivot away and retain the ball. Restrain the aggression of the defender so that the player has an opportunity to learn the moves available using the pivot.

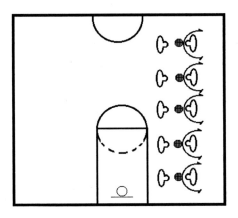

Elementary fake & pivot practice.

Practice shooting without bouncing the ball first. Do not throw away a dribble. What the coach will be looking for here is quickness and dexterity in the movements. These practices will also sharpen the players focus and shooting skills.

Below basket at low post, fake, pivot and put it up. (left & right)

Form two lines of players at forty-five degree angles facing the basket and backboard. Have one player from each line move to the low post, three feet in front of the backboard and outside of the key.

The player will assume the position of having his/her back to the basket. With exaggerated moves fake right, pivot left and put it up with a jump. Each shooter will go for their own rebound and pass it to the next player in line and return to the rear of the line.

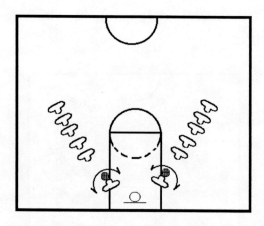

Complete the circuit six times, then repeat the practice with the fake and pivot in the opposite direction. Complete that circuit six times and have the lines switch. Left line is now on the right side and the right side becomes the left side.

Repeat the exercise for the fake, pivot and put it up until all players have had the opportunity to experience shooting from each side of the basket.

At mid-post, fake, pivot and put it up. (left & right)

Form two lines of players at forty-five degree angles facing the basket and backboard. Have one player from each line move to the mid-post, mid way of the lane, in front of the backboard and outside of the key.

The player will assume the position of having his/her back to the basket. With exaggerated moves fake right, pivot left and put it up with a jump. Each shooter will go for their own rebound and pass it to the next player in line and return to the rear of the line.

Complete the circuit three times, then repeat the practice with the fake and pivot in the opposite direction. Complete that circuit three times and have the lines switch. Left line is now on the right side and the right side becomes the left side.

Repeat the exercise for the fake, pivot and put it up until all players have had the opportunity to experience shooting from each side of the basket.

At high post, fake, pivot, break and put it up. (left & right)

Place your player at the top of the key with his/her back to the backboard. Place a second player one step behind the player who will be performing the exercise. Have the player fake to their right, then pivot left, break and put it up. The defender will pivot to go for the rebound and block out the offensive shooter.

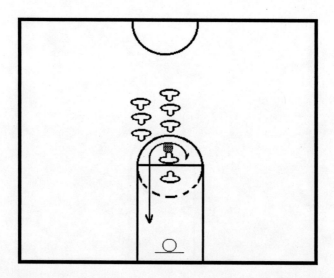

The rebounder passes the ball to the next player in line and the shooter now becomes the defender and the rebounder goes to the back of the shooting line. Complete the circuit five times, then repeat the practice with the fake and pivot in the opposite direction.

Fundamental Rebounding Exercise & Drill.

When rebounding, the player should go up for the rebound, reach for the ball, don't wait for it to come down. It makes no difference whether the rebound is from the offense or defense position, the player must always want possession. The best way to insure success is to go up for the ball.

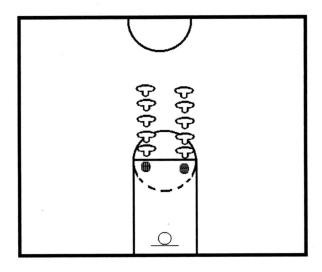

Break your team into two equal sections and have them form a line in front of the basket. The first player in each line stands at the foul shot line and to either side. The object is to put the ball up and have it bounce against the backboard. The right side line shoots to the right of the basket, the left side to the left of the basket.

At the ready signal, the first player in each line will move forward and put the ball up, following it in and going up for the rebound. The player then passes it to the next player in line and returns to the end of the line from which he came. Continue this rotation no less than five times, and until the movement becomes smooth.

Chapter 11

Defense Positions & Moves:

Defense in basketball is the most critical and the most difficult part of the game to play well. The difficulty arises from the fact that defenders are reacting to the situation instead of creating the situation. Defense is forced to become aggressive and act upon disrupting any offensive play by close guarding and always trying to obtain the ball.

To help counteract being in the reactive situation, two basic strategies of defense have been formulated. One is the zone defense, wherein each defender has a pre-defined area or zone to control. He/she then becomes responsible for guarding that area against all intruders. The other is "Man to Man" or called "one on one" defense.

As the coach, I feel you should discuss the following topics with your players in a candid way during discussion breaks in their training. Allow them to understand the overall picture so they individually become aware of how defense is played. Encourage players to get involved with question and answer periods. When they understand the basics of how team defense works, the players get more out of the training session.

Positioning of the zone defensive players is based upon where they are to play in relation to the lane or key. Usually the enter will take a spot above mid-point inside the key, with the forwards just outside of the key on either side of the lane and above the low post. Guards become the forward attack force. Understandably formation definitions have been designated such as the (2-1-2) described above and the (2-3).

One on One defense is pretty much defined by the statement. In this case, each defender becomes responsible for blocking and trapping the offensive player he is assigned. It is one on one basketball which has the possibility of double teaming an offensive player and stripping him of the ball.

Double teaming an offensive player is most often done by the guards in their attempt to funnel the player away from mid court. It happens when an aggressive guard confronts the offense head on, which allows his teammate to sandwich in behind the man with the ball. Offense is now squeezed and a turnover is highly possible by either grabbing the ball or causing a bad pass.

Match Up is the key in man to man defense. You must take into account matching up your players against their opponents on two attributes. Physical size or height and player speed and ability. To have disparity, such as short against tall or slow against quick will blow your defense away.

The primary position on defense is covering the opponent closely keeping them from getting into the key while trying to intercept a pass. If his man has the ball, get between the basket and his man. Move laterally with the man being defended. You must have your center in position to control the key or lane to prevent short jump and lay-up shots.

All players on defense must always be going after the ball when it comes within their reach. Don't guard your assigned man so closely that you allow an offensive player to run right past defense without making an effort to stop him. This happens to often with the younger players who fixate on the man they are guarding. Players on the weak side must back up the defense on the strong side.

This is an effective defense for good or polished players, and requires far more energy to enforce than zone. The weakness of this type of defense shows up when the defense gets spread out, and offense can use effective picks and screens against them. Offense will always have tactics to fit the situation in the advanced teams.

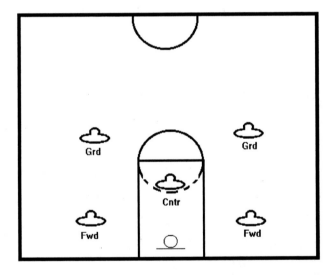

For the younger players, a mix of the two is the easiest to teach and uses the best of both concepts. It becomes a flexible zone defense with the basic (2-1-2) structure. The forwards and center hold man to man in their zone if under pressure. Guards force the play, backed up by zone shifting. When effective, it forces the offense to shoot from a farther distance out.

Weak side, strong side allows the defense their flexibility. Strong side is the side closest to the ball where the defensive players can force the action. Weak side is the positioned players furthest from the ball. Consequently the players on the weak side can reinforce the strong side by closing in on the lane and offensive players.

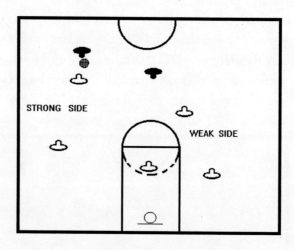

As in most sports, you must act upon the situation to take control, reacting to a situation disadvantages your opportunities to gain control. In basketball, having control of the ball and tactics in mind is a major advantage to the offensive player.

Elementary Defense Practices

Guarding stances and positions against an offensive player.

The proper guarding stance is the same stance we find across the board in sports. The feet are spread apart, the knees are flexed and the body is balanced over the stance's counter-point. Explain to the players that boxing, karate, tennis, football, baseball and basketball all share the common stance. It allows the player to move in any direction quickly by shifting the body balance and foot step.

Lateral movement from the proper stance is also a part of baseball, football, basketball, tennis, and so forth. These are crossover skills that should be explained and demonstrated. In baseball, the infielders must all practice lateral movement to block and catch the ball. They get in front of the ball instead of reaching sideways to catch the ball. Good lateral movement is very important to all the sports.

First illustrate visually what guarding is supposed to be by having a player holding the ball, and a second player facing him with arms out and upwards and using lateral movements to contain the ball carriers progress. In the ideal facing guard position, one hand is raised to block the offenses view of the basket and the other is low to swipe the ball.

Next illustrate visually how to guard the player with the ball who has his/her back towards the guard. The one guarding must not lean into the player but remain within one backwards step of the man with the ball. Again lateral motion is used to keep the offensive player from moving around defense and going for score. Quite often the guard will lean his forearm against the offenses back in order to maintain his position.

Again instruct them to never stand flatfooted and upright when trying to guard. The main key for guarding is in maintaining a good balanced stance with knees flexed. The Guard is then able to move quickly in any direction to contain the offensive player and keep pressure on him. Move like a crab and do it quickly. Make guarding fun.

Elementary Lateral Movement Drill:

Spread the players out and facing the coach. You may choose to have two or more rows depending upon the number of players you have. Have them take the guarding stance. With arms raised and bent at the elbow and hands facing forward and upward, sidestep sideways four steps and reverse direction for four steps. Now increase the number of steps and have the players increase their lateral movement speed.

Next in the process is to add forward and backward movements to the drill. You will lead the drill by facing them and calling for moves to the right, forward, left and back. It's a box pattern which gets everyone working on movements and balance.

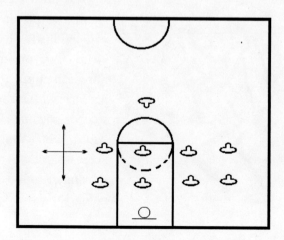

Turn your rows to face each other and repeat the exercise so the players can get the feeling of another person in front of them. It makes it easier for the younger player when defensive moves occur during a scrimmage or game.

Fundamental Lateral Movement Drill:

Spread the players out and facing the coach. You may choose to have two or more rows depending upon the number of players you have. Have them take the guarding stance. With arms raised and bent at the elbow and hands facing forward and upward. This is the same as in the elementary drill, however have them add hustle and quickness.

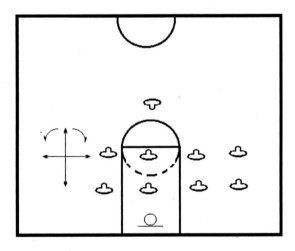

It is performed the same way with forward, backward and sideways movements. The difference is by adding ninety degree pivot to change direction of the guarding movement. Add both left and right pivots and continue in the new direction. Check their feet to make sure they pivot on the outside foot to maintain good balance. Therefore if pivoting to the right it should be made from the left foot.

Grabbing the Ball Drill:

Instruct the team that in this exercise the object is to grab the ball and not the hand or arms of the player with the ball. They should avoid any contact with the other player which could be rendered a foul.

Divide your players into teams of two. Let each team have a basket ball if possible. One player on each team will hold the ball and face the other player standing in front of him. The player with the ball will have four positions in which to move the ball, but not his feet. Positions are to the left, to the right, in front low and overhead. The player without the ball can step one step to the left or one step to the right in order to grab at the ball.

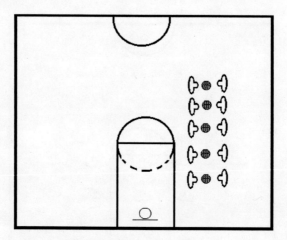

Have the player with the ball move it to his right and the player without the ball take one step and grab it away from the holder. Do not fight over the ball. What is important is where the player places his hands to grab the ball and pull it away. Repeat the drill until all four of the positions have been completed. When this has been accomplished have the players switch rolls and repeat the exercise.

Cycle through the drill several times until the grabber is sure of where to place his hands on the ball to pull it away. Now advise them how during a game or scrimmage that the player with the ball will try hard to hold onto it. In practice, never give the ball away easy. Also in practice grab hard and pull.

Elementary Zone Defense:

In the category I use the (2-1-2) zone and assign the players their respective zone positions and raise their hands above their heads to block the shot. Show them how to move laterally to remain in front of the player with the ball. Teach grabbing for the basketball whenever possible without touching the player. Remember to have the defender pivot around for the rebound if the ball is put up.

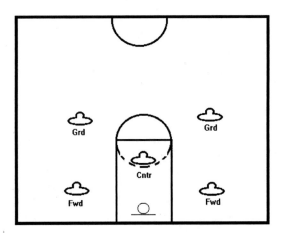

The Exercise.

With positions assigned and their zone pattern established, have your other team members act as offense and attempt to penetrate for a goal. Show defense how to hold their positions in front of the player with the ball. Next use your scrimmage time and whistle to interrupt play and reinforce your instructions. Stress getting to their defensive positions as quickly as they can.

Fundamental Zone Defense:

This configuration is called the (2-3) zone defense. Guards are forward of the key to press offense. The Center guards the key near mid post. The Forwards will be in line with the Center and outside of the key. All of the players remain near or within the three point lane marker. This adds a lot of flexibility for defense to concentrate on opponents coming into their area. Match up can be maintained in the sense of one-on-one.

The Exercise

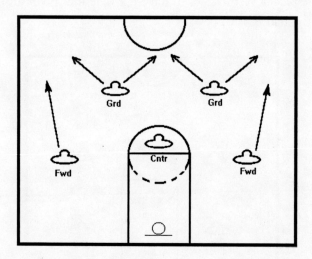

Create two teams for a scrimmage. Each team must be assigned their defensive positions. With your scrimmage underway use the whistle to interrupt play and critique the players performance. Stress getting to their defensive positions as quickly as they can. Encourage offense to open up and attempt to draw defense away from their positions.

Boxing out the offensive players at the key.

The more advanced and capable players must practice blocking out the offense when a ball has been put up. The zone defense is the ideal place to practice this format. However it applies across the line whether zone or man to man. Defense must pivot to face the backboard and place their bodies between the offensive players and the ball.

By facing the backboard they have the advantage in getting the rebound by eliminating the offense from entering the lane area. All players must learn to go up for the rebound. Go to the ball, grab and hold onto the ball, chase for the ball until they get it.

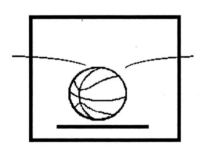

Something to remember when watching the balls flight. A high arc ball will normally rebound short. The shallow flight ball will normally rebound long. Also high arc balls have a better chance of going into the hoop because of the downward kinetics. Balls put up from the right side usually bounce to the left side and vice versa.

Boxing out exercises:

Boxing out exercises are a little too advanced for Categories I & II for a variety of reasons. It may also be considered marginal for kids in the fifth & sixth grades, but begin it there and see how it works with your particular team of players. Remember physical contact is a barrier breaker and touching another person is almost taboo with kids.

1. Break the team into sets of four players. What we are going to do is get familiar with body contact, and the physical feel of boxing another

player out. Try to match the players by size for this drill. Have the players form a box with their backs to each other and pressing against the player behind them. On the count of one, have them push backwards against the player behind them. Allow them to shove and try to hold their positions. On the count of two, have them pivot away from the center of the formation and face each other.

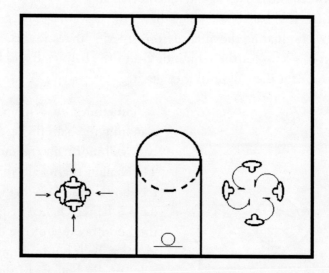

On the count of three, have them pivot back to their starting position and repeat the backward pushing exercise. On the count of four have them pivot away from the center of the formation and face each other.

2. You may break your team up into pairs of two. Give one basketball to each pair on the court. Have the player with the ball turn his back to the other player. Now with both players facing the same way, and the player in front holding the ball forward at arms length and the second player directly behind, have the first player drop the ball.

The job of the second player is to get to the ball, and the first player must block him out. This is where the lateral movement comes into play when the first player moves to restrain the second one, and uses his body to prevent the second player from getting the ball. In simple terms, he butts the second player out.

3. Split you team into two equal numbers of players. One half of the players will form a line at the top of the free throw marker. The other half will be at the end of the lane behind the backboard and directly in line with players above the free throw marker.

Give the ball to the line under the basket. The first player in the line will chest or bounce pass the ball to the player at the free throw line. The objective of this drill is to have the shooter now try to put the ball up as the passer rushes him, causing him to put it up quickly while under assault.

When the passer sees the ball go up, he is to rotate his back to the shooter and block him out from rebounding. The blocker should place himself physically against the shooter to establish his block out. The ball then goes to the next player in the line under the basket.

Use this drill often for the benefit of both the defender and the shooter. Shooting under pressure such as this exercise calls for is one of the best ways to sharpen your shooting drills. Dynamics like this is a great teacher for your teams performance during a game.

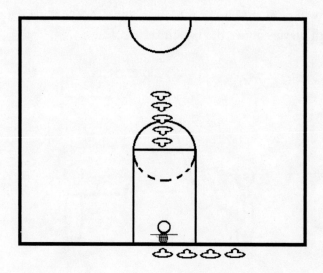

Knowing the trap zones.

The trap zones are in the corners, along the back court line behind the backboard, and down the court side lines. The corner trap is the most difficult to escape from. A player can be trapped by one man and if joined by a second, it's almost always a turnover. And that is due in part upon being unable to pivot away from the defender.

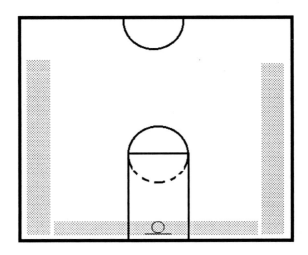

When a player can be forced into a corner, he has lost three quarters of his floor space to escape into. Unable to pivot or break away severely limits where he can pass. When defense can force a man into the corner, do it.

The trap zone along the back court line behind the backboard, limits the player to half of his escape route and makes it impossible to get a shot up. When double teamed under these circumstance, it's almost sure the player will have a turnover. If the defense, while guarding, blocks the ball carriers view with an upheld hand, the man with the ball has an extremely limited chance of getting the ball back into play.

The trap zone along the court side lines, is somewhat like being in the back court situation. It requires two men to trap the ball carrier and force him to the sideline. Again if the defense, while guarding, blocks the ball carriers view with an upheld hand, the man with the ball has an extremely limited chance of getting the ball back into play.

Trapping the offense.

Trapping always requires the defense to force the offensive player with the ball to move towards the sidelines, then double teams him. If offense follows the normal pattern, it will almost always be towards the right side. It seems that right handed dribbling, keeping the ball away from defense, gets itself into this situation. On man to man defense it works the best.

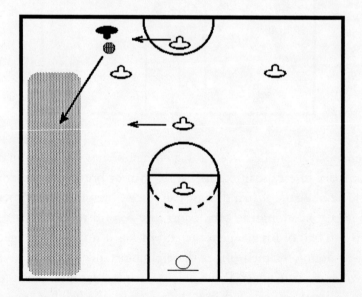

The Exercise requires that we set up a version of the half court press which is a 3-1-1 pattern. Two guards and a power forward make up the

encountering 3. The defender in the center has the task of forcing the offense to move one side or the other.

Depending on the number of players you have, set at least three players above the high point of the key. Have two players bring the ball down in the direction of the basket. The center player of defense will move forward to confront the man with the ball and try to change the offensive mans direction.

Rotate all players through the forward positions to teach them how to effectively move the offense away from the center of the court. Let the players understand that this also works in the back court.

Running defender forces offensive runner towards the side lines.

In the fast break situation, defense must get on the inside of the man running with the ball. When running with an offensive player down court, keep inside, and force him away from the center & basket alignment. If he goes up to shoot, go up with him and block the ball.

The Exercise:

In this exercise, divide your team into two equal groups of players. Place them at the center court line five feet apart. One line will take the ball as the offensive team and the other line will become defense. The objective is to have offense go in for a lay-up and defense to try and move him from his alignment with the basket and block the shot. On "go" have both players run towards the basket for the lay-up. Have the offensive player return to the back of the defense line and the defender to the rear of the offensive line.

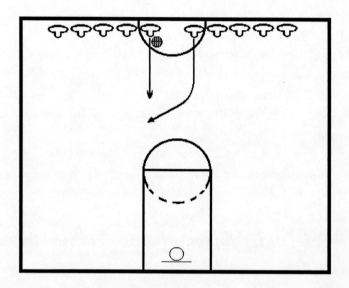

Make several rotations until every player has had the chance to play both positions. Check closely on the lay-up to catch a hand or arm foul and call attention to it. Defense can touch the ball but not the hand or arm.

Going up with offense to block the shot.

The Exercise:

In this exercise, divide your team into two equal groups of players. Place them at the center court line five feet apart. One line will take the ball as the offensive team and the other line will become defense. The objective is to have offense go in for a jump lay-up and defense to try going up with offense and block the shot. On "go" have both players run towards the basket for the lay-up. Have the offensive player return to the back of the defense line and the defender to the rear of the offensive line.

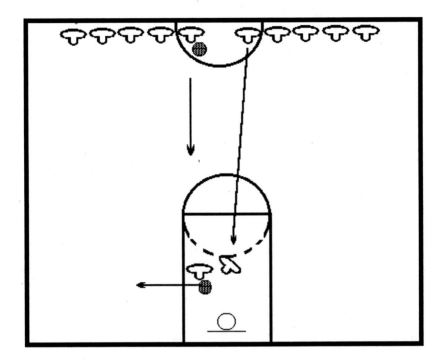

Make several rotations until every player has had the chance to play both positions. Check closely on the lay-up to catch a hand or arm foul and call attention to it. Defense can touch the ball but not the hand or arm.

If your opponent goes up for an overhead pass or shot go UP for the block. Remember in shot blocking to play the ball, not the hand or arm.

Defending against the fast break.

The first and most important option is to pressure the rebounder as quickly as possible. Double team if necessary. Try to force a turnover or prevent the rebounder from making the outlet pass. Secondly you should try to tie up the outlet man who will usually be on the same side of the court as the rebounder.

Guards break to mid court looking for the long pass. They must also run with the breakaway player going down court and attempt to remain between their man and the passer. In effect you are trying to tie up the breakaway players quickly. If running with the player who has the ball, force him away from the basket alignment, if unable to do that, prepare to go up for the rebound. A good fast break is hard to contain, but it can be interrupted if player speed is adequate.

Switching & Talking:

There are no rules against it! Let your players know they can communicate vocally during a scrimmage or game. If a player sees a plan unfolding, let the others know. When a player is picked off or run behind a screen, he should call for a switch, let the others know what is going on. Switching keeps pressure on the man with the ball and makes him have to shoot from further out, or it breaks up a "set" play.

Never switch for just the sake of switching, and when a player does switch have him return to his man as soon as possible. By returning to the player from whom they switched from, the balance of matching up is maintained.

All members on the team should stay alert and automatically make a switch by watching where the ball is, but that's not always the case. A player must be willing and prepared to make the switch. Practice this in your scrimmages.

Talking doesn't apply only to switching, it applies to the turn over as well. If a defender has captured the ball, he should let the rest of the team know it. Whether the man with the ball calls out, "Break" or "Ball" it's telling his team they are on the offensive and they should respond accordingly.

Do's and Don'ts:

Do talk to your teammates about what's going on around you.
Do move to help the team if you are on the weak side.
Do know where the ball is at all times.
Do stay between your opponent and the basket at all times.
Do stay between your man and the opponent with the ball.
Do get into position so you can see the ball handler and your opponent.
Do stay down, with knees bent so you can react, never stand flat footed and straight up, always keep in balance.
Do play your opponent aggressively whether or not he has the ball.
Do attack on defense, make the ball handler commit himself.
Do recover quickly on a turnover, know what you have to do.
Do switch when necessary and let your teammates know it.
Do get back on a fast break and pick up the player nearest you.
Do go with the dribbler and steal the ball if it's on your side.
Do force your opponent to move laterally and away from the basket, try to put him in the corner or along the sidelines.
Do pick up your man as quickly as possible and keep him away from the area he wants.
Do annoy your opponent, keep your hands and arms moving to distract the ball handler.

Do box out your man the moment the ball goes up. Box out your opponent first, then go for the rebound.
Don't leave the back court uncovered when your team shoots.
Don't play the ball if you have a weak defense, play the man.

Chapter 12

Playing the Offense

Playing the offense is the fun part of the game. Possession of the all and wanting to score is the "high" of basketball. Everyone sees themselves as goal makers. Watching children on the schools outdoor courts is a good indicator of what they want to do. Each boy or girl will put the ball up the moment they get it. It's school yard scrimmage, and lots of fun. We should attempt to keep the fun in the game when teaching children how it's played.

Let them know that offense has a decided advantage on court. Offense is acting upon the game and not reacting to it. The team in possession should hold onto and move the ball around until the best shot opportunity for a player is found. Each player should be encouraged that he can and must put the ball up when he has a good shot opportunity. No risk, no reward.

If you insist that the player takes his chances when a good opportunity presents itself, you have taken the burden of a missed shot from his shoulders and placed it upon your own. The key word here is a good shot "opportunity". The ideal situation is when the player is in a good floor position and unchallenged by a defender.

The team can be instructed about how setting screens is to the offense as boxing out is to the defense. Any player may set a screen. The legal screen is an action by a player who, without causing contact, delays or prevents an opponent from reaching a desired position. He/she may face any direction. The Screener must be stationary, except when both players are moving in the same path and same direction.

What this means to the player is that during play, you may block out a defender by taking a stationary position in front of him to prevent him from attacking the player with the ball. You can face him or turn your back to him. This in turn allows the player with the ball to approach his shot from behind a screen and put it up.

The moving screen is when one player with the ball is running down court and closely followed by a second player who prevents the player with the ball from being over taken by a defender. An example would be found in the fast break where an offensive player has broken for a lay-up, and his teammate runs just behind and inside of the man with the ball. If the screen slows or stops and contact is made with a defender, the defender is at fault and subject to a foul.

A **pick** is a player, stationary in position, who may be brushed against or run closely past by the man with the ball. What the man with the ball is doing is running the man guarding him into a wall while he escapes to make a play. Teach the team that setting a pick is much like setting a screen. By using a stationary teammate as a pick to rid the ball handler of the player guarding him, gives the offense another tool for scoring.

Offensive rebounding instruction is a must for the winning team. A player who puts the ball up, must follow it in for the rebound. Whenever a ball is put up, it is normal for everyone to watch the flight of the ball. It is during that "spectator" period that the offense must move past the defense and attempt to box them out. Always assume that the ball will rebound and go for it.

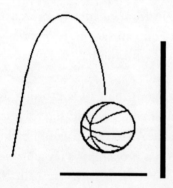

There are several characteristics associated with a balls flight that should be explained. A high arc ball will normally rebound short. Also high arc balls have a better chance of going into the hoop because of the downward ballistics. The shallow flight ball will normally rebound long and back to the shooter. Seventy percent of shots made from the left side with high arc bounce to the right side when missed. This also applies to shots made from the right side bouncing to the left side.

Because these characteristics hold true, most forwards position themselves on either side of the basket and relatively close in on both offense and defense. The taller children on these young teams will normally be assigned as forwards, and then "posted up" during scrimmage or game play. Their position is known as "low post" which is close in to the backboard. If the forward gets the ball during defense, he is now set up for the fast break.

The fast break is designed for offense to get the ball to the goal before the opposing defense can be established. The play is triggered by a good rebounder who can get the ball out to another player quickly. The player receiving the ball from the rebounder is considered the outlet man. He may break down-court or pass to another player ahead of him. It's normal for the point guard to make the down-court break as soon as the ball has been retrieved by his teammate.

If more than one player is making the down-court break, the ball should be passed between them, allowing the most mid court player to select the man to make the lay-up, or do it himself. The passing puts pressure on the defense who will be trying to break up the run.

Our players in **Category I** and **Category II** are capable of doing some of this work, but not much of it. Be patient and let them have fun when you are explaining some of the advanced movements in the game. Forget about having the little people working on jump shots, have them shoot from a good balanced open position. Let them find for themselves their own shooting range and practice it.

Youngsters have a tendency to almost without exception dribble themselves into the right hand corner of the court or along the right sideline. This is a natural phenomenon since they try to dribble with the hand away from the defender, and most dribble right handed. This is when you can show them the dangers of the trap zones.

It's easily demonstrated when you take them to the sidelines and illustrate how they have lost half of the court for movement. Then take them into the corner and show them how they've lost three quarters of the court for movement. When trapped or double teamed, young players go to ground when trying to protect the ball from a turnover. They will clutch it tight and hold it low which is the wrong thing to do, but that is how it is with youngsters. Don't force the issue here.

In **Categories III** and **IV** offense takes a major jump. This is when we can begin developing the very foundation of offensive play by introducing the give and go routines. Give and go develops into what are termed "set plays", and these are taught from high school through the professionals. These categories of players can also learn how to get off the floor by going up for shooting, rebounding and passing.

If we can assume they understand the trap zones, then you must show them how to go up and over the defenders with either the overhead pass or the hook pass to get out of trouble. Most players have a tendency to stay to low with the ball which can be grabbed by the defense resulting in a turnover. The overhead pass offers a variety of options for faking and breaking.

There are three basic passes used most of the time. The chest pass, the bounce pass and the overhead pass. There is a simple axiom that applies here. "Fake a pass to make a pass." Consider how the overhead pass is used to illustrate this point. The man with the ball feints raising it for making an overhead pass with the defender going up with his arms to block the pass. As defense goes up he pulls it down and bounce passes around him, or makes a break away from the defender.

Creating misdirection is one of offenses major tools. That's why offense has such an advantage on court. Some of your younger players will pick up feinting with the ball quickly. For the girls who play it's a matter of finesse, for the boys, a form of taunting. In any case it's very important for the older children to adopt feinting in their play. In a way, faking out the opponent is a double edged sword which works for both offense and defense. A defender may also mislead his opponent with his intentions.

Note: Always use the fast break during practice scrimmages.

Do's and don'ts.

Always be in balance when shooting during practice or play.
Always put the ball up when you have a good shot possibility.
Always look at the basket whenever you are shooting.
Always Follow your shot in for the rebound.
Always Grab the basketball whenever possible.
Always scramble hard for the rebounds-offensive or defensive.
Move quickly and pass quickly when setting up for shots.
Always look at your pass receiver when passing.
Know who has the ball, and make an effort to assist.
Keep the ball low when dribbling.

Always attempt box out the defense when your team shoots.
Don't hold onto the ball so long as to be trapped by the
opponent.
Don't look at the ball when dribbling, instead of the court.

The following drills and exercises are designed for training the young players in how to play offense. These are only drills and not the only ones which you can use. Your creative input with new and different methods will certainly be of benefit to your kids. You may modify any of the following to fit your needs and please do so when you feel it is in your teams best interest.

Pivot-break and pass across (bounce or chest)

Form two lines of players. One line will be above the key and to the right of the lane. The other line shall be at mid post outside of the key on the left side facing the key. The lines are now at 90 degrees to each other and separated by the width of the lane and the distance between the high and mid post.

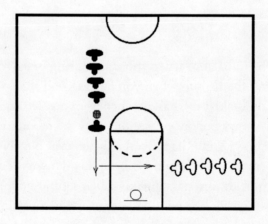

Have the first player in the line facing the basket, take the ball and turn his back to the backboard. With exaggerated moves, fake right, pivot left and break towards the backboard and passing to the first player in the mid post line. Simulates a Guard breaking into the key and passing to a Forward.

The receiver passes the ball to the top line and goes to the end f the breaking line. The passer returns to the rear of the receivers line. Complete that circuit six times and have the lines switch. Left line is now on the right side and the high post to the top left side.

Repeat the exercise for the fake, pivot and pass until all players have had the opportunity to experience breaking from each side of the top of the key post.

Pivot-break and pass across & receiver puts it up.

Form two lines of players. One line will be above the key and to the right of the lane. The other line shall be at mid post outside of the key on the left side facing the key. The lines are now at 90 degrees to each other and separated by the width of the lane and the distance between the high and mid post.

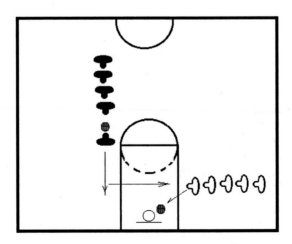

Have the first player in the line facing the basket, take the ball and turns his back to the backboard. With exaggerated moves, fake right, pivot left and break towards the backboard and passing to the first player in the mid post line. Simulates a Guard breaking into the key and passing to a Forward.

The receiver, without a dribble, puts the ball up and follows it in for the rebound. The receiver passes the ball to the top line and goes to the end of the breaking line. The passer returns to the rear of the receivers line. Complete that circuit six times and have the lines switch. Left line is now on the right side and the high post to the top left side.

Repeat the exercise until all players have had the opportunity to experience breaking from each side of the top of the key post.

Offense/defense lay-up practice on the run

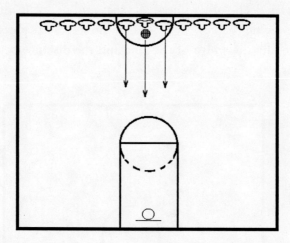

In this exercise, divide your team into two equal groups of players. Place them behind the center court line five feet apart. The objective is to allow each player to be either offense or defense depending on who gets the ball. We are practicing both offense and defense at the same time while going for a lay-up. Toss the ball forward of the center line with a high arc. When the ball touches the floor, have a player from each line scramble forward to get the ball and continue in for a lay-up.

Offense when running with the ball, must dribble with the hand away from the defense. Have the play continue until one of the players has been able to make a basket. Each player will return to the end of the line from which they started from. You can add competition by giving score to each line for their players basket.

Fake, pivot and put it up. (left & right)

Form two lines of players at forty-five degree angles facing the basket and backboard. Have one player from each line move to the low post, three feet in front of the backboard and outside of the key.

The player will assume the position of having his/her back to the basket. With exaggerated moves fake right, pivot left and puts it up with a jump. Each shooter will go for their own rebound and pass it to the next player in their line and return to the rear of the line.

Complete the circuit six times, then repeat the practice with the fake and pivot in the opposite direction. Complete that circuit six times and have the lines switch. Left line is now on the right side and the right side becomes the left side.

Repeat the exercise for the fake, pivot and put it up until all players have had the opportunity to experience shooting from each side of the basket.

Running pivot past defender.

Split your team into two equal numbers and have them form into two lines allowing at least six feet of separation between each player in both lines. Have the two line face each other from approximately twelve feet apart. Each player in the action line will have a ball. Each player in the defense line will assume the guarding position.

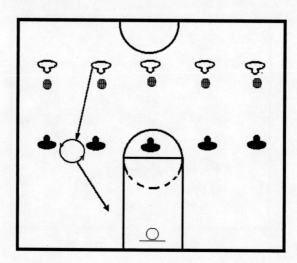

The ball carrier now dribbles towards the defender, on approach, pivots a 360 and cuts to the right side with the ball being dribbled in the hand away from the defender. Defender is allowed to move laterally two steps. Initially have the players with the balls walk through the exercise and instruct them in how to pivot away. Repeat the cycle five times then reverse handler and defender.

Setting a screen.

Split your team into two equal numbers and form one group into a zone defense pattern around and in the lane for demonstration purposes. Place the other team members peripherally outside of the defense zone. Have a Guard with the ball move towards mid post and the Forward on that side move in and take a guarding position between the ball carrier and his selected man.

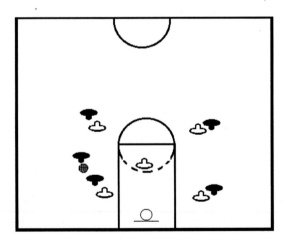

With the Screen in place, have the Guard move in an up with a shot over his screen and the defender. With this established, have each player on the offensive team take a screening position on the player nearest to themselves. Next reverse offense and defense and repeat the positions so each player understands what a screen does on offense.

Setting a pick.

Set four players outside of the lane. Two will represent defense and two will represent offense. Have defense aligned between offense and the basket for demonstration purposes. Position them at high post and mid post on the right side of the lane. With offense at high post handling the ball, have the player fake to his left then break right past mid post offense using him as a pick and cutting for the basket.

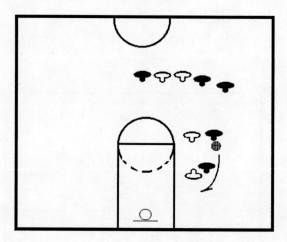

Next reverse offense and defense and repeat the positions until each of the four players understands what a pick does on offense. Continue alternating your players into these positions until each team player understands the job of the pick and how it works. Every member of the team will be capable of setting either a pick or a screen.

Rebounding Shooting Drill at Low Post.

Using the backboard is essential to improving the probability of making a goal. And in this drill, the player must use the backboard every time he puts the ball up. It requires that each player in turn, moves to the low post just inside and to the right of the key. This is the position where a player is most likely to get his rebound. Have the player put the ball up for a goal using the backboard.

He takes his own rebound, shifts to the left side of the basket just inside of the key and shoots for his goal using the backboard. He will continue to alternate sides and shoot as long as he makes a goal using the backboard. When he misses, he returns to the rear of the line and the next player steps forward to repeat the exercise.

Each player will continue shooting until he misses. When the player can score ten (10) consecutive goals while alternating sides, he is considered competent. As the players improve, have them pick up the pace while shifting from side to side and rebounding. Use this drill often to sharpen their scoring.

You may add an additional touch if you choose, and that would be to move the player two or more additional steps away from the backboard and repeat the same drill using the backboard.

A Game called "21".

We are always looking for drills and exercises that will aid the players in developing their individual skills. "21" is a game which uses three players and one goal. It is basically each man playing for himself against the other players. What we accomplish with this type of drill is dribbling, ball handling, feinting or faking, shooting from every position on the floor near the goal, rebounding, foul shots and the three point long ball.

I believe that you can start the youngsters as early as the third grade in playing the game, for it's a lot like school yard basketball. It differs only when we add the foul shot and long ball shots after each goal is made. Children love the game and never realize they are building their skills. It's also your opportunity to teach them how to "fake a shot to make a shot."

The restrictions you put on the players are the same they will have during a scrimmage or game. No traveling, no double dribble, don't foul the shooter, the player who loses the ball out of court cannot be the one to retrieve it and begin again and no wrestling over the ball. A player fouled gets two free throws. Don't allow helter skelter running all over the court to the mid court line. Instead they must remain within the proximity of the three point marker.

Scoring is straight forward and simple. A goal is two points, foul shots are one point each, and the long ball is three points. A boy who makes a goal is given two free throw shots. If he makes the first one, and misses the second, the ball is back in play. If he misses the first he gets a second shot. If he makes the second shot the ball is back in play and may be rebounded by any player.

If the player makes both foul shots, he then moves to the three point line for a long ball attempt. Whether the player makes or misses the long shot, the ball is back in play again and anyone may rebound it including the shooter. To extend the play you adjust how the score accumulates. To begin with, a player can get two points for his goal, two for foul shots and three for the three pointer which is a total of seven points.

If a player reaches a score where three or less points are needed to win, the final shot must be from behind the three point line. The player who has twenty points will receive no points for a goal made, but is given the opportunity to put up the three pointer to win. What is sometimes done to extend the game, is to have the player who misses a potential win with the three pointer to reduce his score to fifteen and begin building again.

When a player has won, he steps out of the game and you allow the other two to finish. This game may be as flexible as you want it to be for the players you have and at what level they are playing.

The game is an excellent platform for you to coach them on going up for the rebound, faking a shot and breaking away to find a better position to shoot from and improve concentration on the game. If your players get accustomed to shooting under pressure, they will become better players during a game. The foul shots are also under pressure which simulates game pressure.

As a final remark concerning "21", and the number of players you put on the floor. It is possible to play four players by playing two on two. Scoring remains the same with regards to making a three point finisher, however the three pointer can be made from the court as a goal. By that, instead of having to make a two point goal to get the long ball opportunity, the players can go directly to the long ball from the court for a winner.

Whether you play two on two or three on three, you can coach the players on passing, assisting and working on give'n goes. This can be a real help as you build towards team performance. You use only half the court, keeping the players in close with man-to-man as your defense. You also level the playing ground using the scoring method as opposed to scrimmage scoring.

Building the Give and Goes.

This is where we begin to tie all of the drill elements together in the playing of the game. The passing, shooting, dribbling, ball handling, setting picks and setting a screen drills bring us to this point. Give and goes are the keys to playing basketball. We will begin with the A, B, C's of give and goes. To define this, it is simply one player passing off to another who returns it to the first player who will go for a shot. It becomes more complex as we expand on it, but never the less, that's what it's about.

A "give'n go" requires the cooperation of two or more players in setting up to score. It demands "teamwork" from all players that are involved. Until this begins to happen, the players primarily play a form of school yard scrimmage. With younger children that's about as good as it will get, however kids eight and up should be able to pick up on simple forms of exchange that will work on many occasions.

One further suggestion I'd like to make concerning the following drills, is to have the players who are shooting in close to use the backboard. If they have the agility, have them go up for the shot and get above the court. The shot now becomes a "touch" shot which is easier than an "on deck" shot.

High to Low Post Give and Go-Both Sides

Place a forward outside of the key ahead of the backboard and just below mid post. Have the other players beyond the three point marker. Have the first player in the line break forward and snap a high pass to the receiver who goes up for the ball, takes it, and snaps a pass back to the incoming player who cuts in for a lay-up.

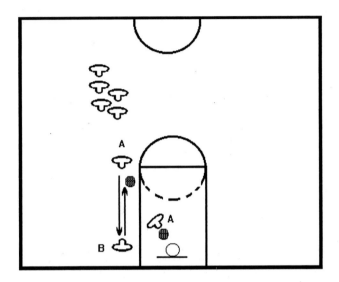

In this case "A", moving forward passes to "B" who instantly puts is back to "A" who has cut in for a lay-up. "A" gets his own rebound and passes it to the next man in line and then returns to the back of the line. If you have enough players you may run two lines, one on either side of the key. After three cycles, you can switch them from left side to right side and vice versa. I would suggest that you rotate all of your players into the forward position when time allows over several sessions.

High to Low Post Give and Screen-Both Sides

Place a forward outside of the key ahead of the backboard and just below mid post. Have the other players beyond the three point marker. Have the first player in the line break forward and snap a high pass to the receiver who goes up for the ball and takes it. The passer continues in as if to receive a pass but becomes a screen on the defender. The receiver pivots out and behind his screen and puts the ball up over the screen. The man setting the screen must then box out defense to complete the effort.

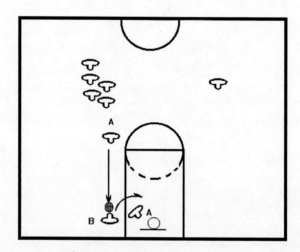

In this case "A", moving forward passes to "B" who goes up for the ball, feints left then breaks right going behind "A" who has set a screen. "A" gets the rebound and passes it to the next man in line and then returns to the back of the line. If you have enough players you may run two lines, one on either side of the key. After three cycles, you can switch them from left side to right side and vice versa. I would suggest that you rotate all of your players into the pivot position when time allows over several sessions.

High to Low Post Give and Go Go-Both Sides

Place a forward outside of the key ahead of the backboard and just below mid post. Have the other players beyond the three point marker. Have the first player in the left line break forward and snap a high pass to the forward who goes up for the ball, takes it, and snaps a pass back to the incoming player across the key on the right side who goes in for a lay-up.

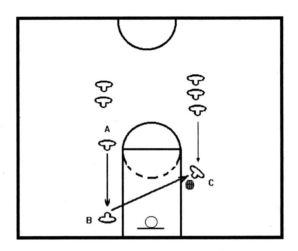

In this case "A", moving forward passes to "B" who instantly snaps it to "C" who has cut in for a lay-up. "C" gets his own rebound and passes it to the next man in the starting line and then returns to the back of the starting line while "A" goes to the back of the put up line. After three cycles, you can switch them from left side to right side. I would suggest that you rotate all of your players into the forward's position when time allows over several sessions.

Mid to Mid Post Give and Go-Both Sides

Place a forward outside of the key and located near mid post. Have the other players beyond the three point marker near the sideline. Have the first player in the line break forward and snap a high pass to the receiver who goes up for the ball, takes it, and snaps a pass back to the incoming player who goes in for a lay-up.

In this case "A", moving forward passes to "B" who instantly puts is back to "A" who has cut in for a lay-up. "A" gets his own rebound and passes it to the next man in line and then returns to the back of the line. If you have enough players you may run two lines, one on either side of the key. After three cycles, you can switch them from left side to right side and vice versa. I would suggest that you rotate all of your players into the forward position when time allows over several sessions.

Mid to Mid Post Give and Screen-Both Sides

Place a forward outside of the key and located near mid post. Have the other players beyond the three point marker near the sideline. Have the first player in the line break forward and snap a high pass to the receiver who goes up for the ball and takes it. The passer continues in as if to receive a pass but becomes a screen on the defender. The receiver pivots out and behind his screen and puts the ball up over the screen. The man setting the screen must then box out defense to complete the effort.

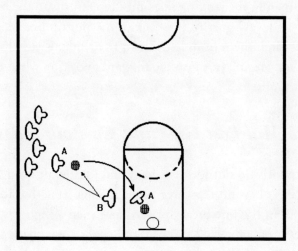

In this case "A", moving forward passes to "B" who goes up for the ball, feints left then breaks right going behind "A" who has set a screen. "A" gets the rebound and passes it to the next man in line and then returns to the back of the line. If you have enough players you may run two lines, one on either side of the key. After three cycles, you can switch them from left side to right side and vice versa. I would suggest that you rotate all of your players into the pivot position when time allows over several sessions.

High Post Give and Goes-Both Sides.

Place a player at the foul shot line facing toward mid court. Near mid court form your players in a line. Place yourself directly behind the pivot man to direct him with what you want him to be doing.

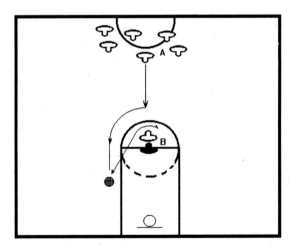

The first player "A" in the line will dribble forward, passing to the Pivot man "B", fakes left, then cuts right around the high post towards the basket. "B" feints right, pivots left and returns the pass to the first player who goes in for a lay-up. In returning the ball to the first player, he continues his motion around the defender getting behind him and boxing him out of the play

The shooter will rebound the ball and pass it to the first player at the mid court line, and assume the pivots position at the foul shot line. The pivot man will return to the end of the shooters line. Rotate all players through five cycles. At completion of the cycles, reverse the cut around from right side to left side and repeat.

High Post Give and Screen-Both Sides.

Place a player at the foul shot line facing toward mid court. Near mid court form your players in a line. Place yourself directly behind the pivot man to direct him with what you want him to be doing.

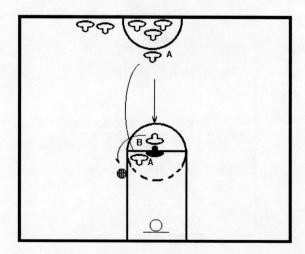

The first player "A" in the line will dribble forward, passing to the Pivot man "B", then cuts right around "B" towards the basket and sets a screen for "B". "B" feints right, pivots left and breaks in for a lay-up. "A" is now in position to box out the defense that was on "B".

The shooter will rebound the ball and pass it to the first player at the mid court line. "A" will assume the pivots position at the foul shot line. Rotate all players through five cycles. At completion of the cycles, reverse the cut around from right side to left side and repeat.

High Post Give and Go Go-Both Sides.

Place a player at the foul shot line facing toward mid court. Near mid court form your players in two lines. Place yourself directly behind the pivot man to direct him with what you want him to be doing. Have the first player in the left line break forward and snap a pass to the pivot who feints left then snaps a pass to the incoming player on the right side who goes in for a lay-up.

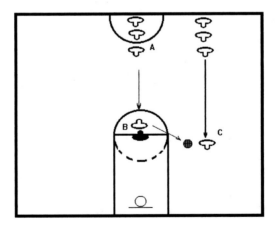

In this case "A", moving forward passes to "B" who instantly snaps it to "C" who has cut in for a lay-up. "C" gets his own rebound and passes it to the next man in the starting line and then returns to the back of the starting line while "A" goes to the back of the put up line. After three cycles, you can switch them from left side to right side. I would suggest that you rotate all of your players into the pivot position when time allows over several sessions.

High Post Give and Go Options-Both Sides

Place a player at the foul shot line facing toward mid court. Near mid court form your players in two lines. Set two players at low post, one on either side of the key. Have the first player in the left line break forward and snap a pass to the pivot who feints left then snaps a pass to the incoming player on the right side who now exercises the option of either passing to the man across the key or to the player directly in front of him. The option receiver feints away from the basket, then pivots and without a dribble puts the ball up. It is rebounded by "C" and passed to the top of the starting line.

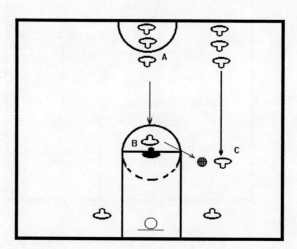

When the right side has completed it's option cycle, switch to the left side and have them complete an option cycle. Rotate out the players playing pivot and low post and start over again until all players have had a chance to be in the pivot position.

Review Summary about Give and Goes.

At this point we have set precedents to promote teamwork in order to create team scores. Although the players have been given these practice drills, they must also understand that during a game, all players must work to set the play in motion. As an example, the player at low post may be closely guarded. When he receives a hand signal of intent for a give and go, it is his responsibility to break out to receive the pass, then put it into play.

I would like to suggest that you put your offensive players in position with a defender near each man. Walk them through the exercise you want executed, showing each man his options for breaking out to get the ball. Assume a forward is near low post and outside of the key. The guard, just inside of the three point marker and on the right side gives his hand signal A defender is between the forward and the guard. If the forward cuts towards the basket, receives the pass which he returns to the guard, he is now in perfect position to box out his defender.

Everyone is involved when we take these basics and begin to make "set plays". In a "set play" each man on the floor has a job to perform, whether it is boxing out for offensive rebounding or breaking away to pull his defense man away from the action.

"Breaking Away" is also used by an offensive player to get loose from his defender when defense is playing "man to man". It happens when he feints one direction, then breaks to be open in the other. This is often done in higher level play. It allows the breaking player the opportunity to receive the ball and initiate a give and go, or to put the ball up by charging the lane.

The "Breaking" signal may be given by the player who wants to receive the ball or by the player who has the ball. If it is called by the player with the ball, all players on his team immediately "break" to be open to receive a pass and get the ball in motion. By the time most players reach the eighth grade level, this will have become a playing habit and will not require hand signals.

Developing A "Set Play."

Your team is now at the point where their exposure to moving the ball around with give and goes allows them a new dimension in the game. They can begin to plan and develop a method for attacking their opponents defense. You should encourage them in every way to make a "set play" their own. Help them to design a play they feel will work, them allow them to put it to test during a practice or league game.

All "set plays" are based on "give'n go" tactics. All have options built into them. What is important is developing the players willingness to make the "team" effort and strengthen the bond among themselves. You may start with a simple Hi Post give and go using the scissor moves around the top of the key with the forwards moving in to box out the defense.

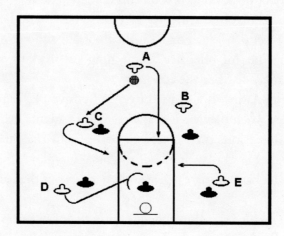

As we get into tactics, we'll cover more of the "set plays" and how they work. Some of the "set plays" have become standards in college and pro basketball. Although we are covering this type of material, I do not mean to imply that your children will convert to its use easily. Some of the older players will pick up on the subject but the little players will have difficulty.

It does not hurt for he youngest of players to be informed, as a matter or fact it helps them to feel knowledgeable. Even if they are unable to do these things they like knowing about it.

Chapter 13

Strategies & Tactics

Strategy is the generalship of the game, the overall view of the game at hand. Tactics are the moves and positioning of the players during the game to obtain their objectives. An example might be that a team you are going to play is known for it's fast break offense. Your strategy then is to nullify that portion of their game. You may then employ tactics to stifle the fast break. The tactics are to swarm the rebounder and cut off the outlet man.

What you will most likely encounter are teams who have one or more players who can handle a ball reasonably well with some shooting skills. These boys are the ones who will be supported by the lesser players of the team, and fed most of the balls. That will require your players to closely guard their key player to nullify what they will consider an advantage.

Since we are dealing with youngsters from as young as five and a half to boys or girls almost sixteen, we are not going to explore formations and tactics that apply to high school and beyond. We are going to cover some of the basic elements of "set" plays, and have you build upon them with players of your team.

Explain how Strategy and Tactics apply to both offensive and defensive play and formations. All of the practices and drills have led us to this point where we now begin to play the game with "set plays". These are definable in almost simple diagrams and their variations are nearly endless. What makes it work is clever and clean performance and execution.

Obviously the more we practice and play the better the performance and execution. This is all built on the basics of the game. If you know and can perform the basics well, "set plays" will almost evolve by themselves. I suggest that you allow your young players to devise some of the tactics and add excitement to their game. But more than that, what you are doing is making them and yourself into a team.

When your team begins to build on the basic tactics, keep an open mind to their suggestions. Try to promote this involvement with your team, which in turn results in their focus on the game. Intelligent play within a team goes a long way towards winning. Consider using this at half time during a practice or league game. Ask the players for input whether or not your team is winning or losing.

As the coach, you're responsible for getting an overview of what is taking place on the court. You must make the choices for the tactics that you need to implement. However, in the huddle, state what you think must be done and allow feedback from your players. The decision of course is yours, and you have the final say, but allow participation.

Offensive Movements and Positions of Responsibility.

The game is based upon movement, continuous flow, and circulation for the team with the ball. The offensive players who are without the ball circulate within a particular area and keep the defense busy trying to interrupt a set play or passing attempt. Each player without the ball, and moving in his general area of responsibility, should expect to receive the ball when he is open.

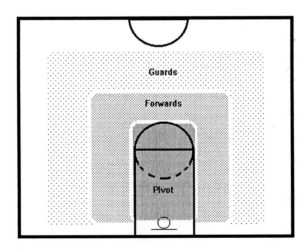

Guards play further out and normally shoot the longer ball. Forwards and the Center or pivot man make most of the lay-ups and shorter shots. Guards should practice from 15 to 24 feet, forwards and centers should concentrate in the 12 to 20 feet. That does not mean that Guards are restricted from lay-ups or Forwards are confined to only shorter shots. By being in motion and able to cut to the ball, this makes it difficult for defense. It also spreads defense out and gives offense more opportunities.

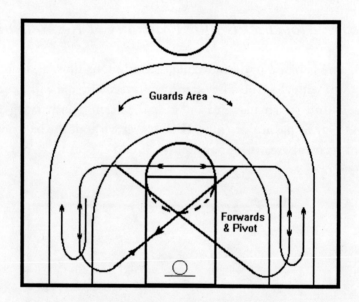

Now, with defense spread, cutting lines open, offense is in a better position for getting the rebound. No one is starting from a dead motion position to charge the backboard. Don't forget the tap-in, when open under the backboard with a good chance of making it, do it.

Full court presses and how they work.

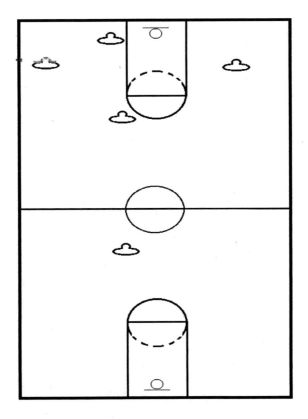

This calls for three men forward with two men back. This is a 3-1-1 zone type formation. Pressure is put on the in-bounding player by playing him closely, and the two backup men are set to double team a receiver or intercept the ball. One possibility is to cause the 5 second turnover delay and get the ball out of bounds. Once the ball is in-bounded, the man guarding the in-bounder stays close to him in the event of a return pass.

The man playing short safety between foul line and mid-course line looks to intercept the outlet pass. Deep safety protects his court from the mid-course line to the basket. He looks to intercept a hurried pass from far court to his area. If the offense manages to break out, the team now picks up the nearest man for one on one defense. In every press situation you want to keep the ball along the side lines or in the trap zone as much as possible and out of mid court.

Half court presses and how they work.

This calls for three men forward with two men back. This is a 3-1-1 zone type formation. Pressure is put on the incoming player by playing his closely and forcing him away from center court. The two backup men are set to double team the dribbler or intercept the ball. The object is to force the man to lose his dribble or shoot from outside.

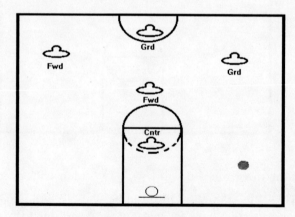

The man playing short safety is at the foul line and looks to intercept a pass or pressure a pass receiver. Deep safety protects his zone from the mid-post line to the basket. He looks to intercept a hurried pass from far court to his area. If the offense manages to break out, the team now picks up the nearest an for one on one defense.

Attacking the Full Court Press.

The in-bounding play against the full court press calls for a spread out box formation. Each intended receiver fakes for misdirection, then moves to find an open spot as indicated. The player making the in-bound pass then sprints down-court looking to convert the press into a fast break situation. The team, with a minimum of dribbling wants to quickly follow the in-bounding player and try to establish a three man attack pattern against the two man defense under the basket. The ball should be moved down court by passing between the attack players.

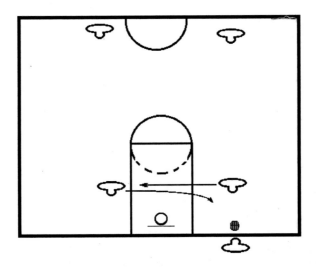

On some occasions the in-bound receivers under full court press will break two men mid-course and two men between the foul line and the forecourt line. The player passing the ball in, uses the baseball pass and puts it over the heads of defense and down-court for a fast break. This calls for a quick start by the receivers.

In-bounding formulas for Out-Of-Bounds plays.

First, consider the five (5) second turnover time delay. This can be avoided if you have a plan for putting the ball into play. Secondly if you are breaking a full court press, and thirdly you are under your opponents basket. Last but not least is in-bounding from the sideline. Some teams become so rattled by aggressive defending at the line that they either lose possession of the ball by time delay, or make a pass to a player that is covered for a turnover.

There are basically two in-bounding patterns used to get the ball into play. They are the box and the line formations. When and how they are employed depends on whether you are in-bounding from under the basket or along the sidelines. To start the in-bounding play, the player with the ball makes sure his team is in position, then calls "Break". On command the players go into action.

The player who is responsible for putting the ball in is under pressure from a defender who often flags wildly in his attempt to knock the ball off kilter, or prevent him from having an open target. It's up to him to find the open man and get the ball into play before the clock runs out, then break into court where he may be available to receive a return pass.

Within the in-bounding procedures, players may set screens and picks to facilitate the formations success. Often the player who passes the ball in will cut for a return pass, pivot and put it up. Getting the ball into play without a turnover is almost always assured if the formations have been practiced.

In-bounding from under the basket-Box

Player "A" will pass on the "Break" call to "C" who has feinted in the direction of the basket, then cut around "B" who has moved to set a screen where "C" was. "D" and "E" have made the same moves as "B" and "C" in the front. "A" is now open and goes to the middle of the lane for a return pass and lay-up. If "C" is closed on the move, then "E" will be open. The intention here is to go for an in close basket.

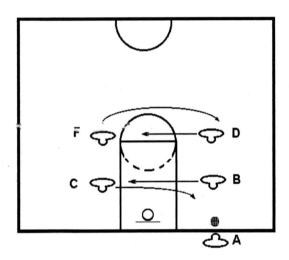

Set your players on the court in these positions and have them at the "Break" call out, perform the drill and put the shot up. Rotate each of the team players through each position until they understand how each position works. Every player should be capable of taking any of the positions and making it work.

In-bounding from under the basket-Line

Player "A" must choose the open man as quickly as possible, and it will normally be either "B" or "C" who are in the best position to put it up quickly. "B" is cutting inside to mid-post in the lane, "C" breaks towards the corner, "D" cuts in and down towards "A" and "E" goes out at high post to receive. Therefore one man has cut inside and two have cut outside with one approaching the in-bounding player. Once the ball is released, "A" cuts to the foul shot lane.

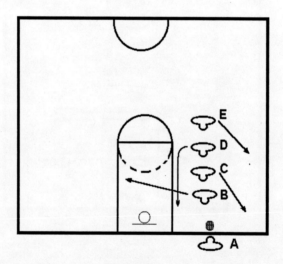

Set your players on the court in these positions and have them at the "Break" call out, perform the drill and put the shot up. Rotate each of the team players through each position until they understand how each position works. Every player should be capable of taking any of the positions and making it work.

In-bounding from under the basket-Line (Reverse)

This pattern is just the reverse of the one previously shown. All players move in the opposite direction from what the "Break" call triggered. Therefore right moves to the left and left moves to the right. The intent is to not allow defense to get accustomed to your formation and neutralize it. Once the ball is released, "A" cuts to the foul shot lane.

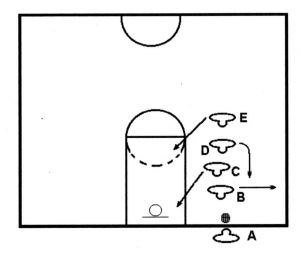

Set your players on the court in these positions and have them at the "Reverse" call out, perform the drill and put the shot up. Rotate each of the team players through each position until they understand how each position works. Every player should be capable of taking any of the positions and making it work.

In-bounding from the side court-Line

From the formation shown, the out-of-bounds passer will pick up a screen or pick and break for the basket. He is joined there in a scissors action by player "C" who feints and cuts around after reversing himself. Player "B" now has the options of passing to either men at mid-post or the two nearest him. If open, moves in for a lay-up using the in-bounder and "C" as screens.

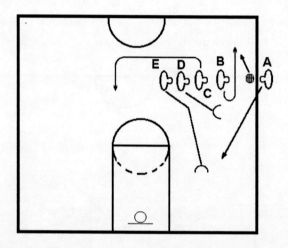

Set your players on the court in these positions and have them at the "Break" call out, perform the drill and put the shot up. Rotate each of the team players through each position until they understand how each position works. Every player should be capable of taking any of the positions and making it work.

In-bounding from the side court-Tandem 4 across.

In this situation the players line up parallel to the sideline of the court and in line to move towards the basket. This formation opens a lot of new possibilities for a frontal attack using picks and screens against an extended defense.

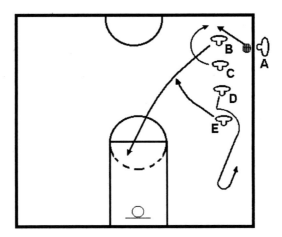

Each player has a concept of where he should go and what he should be doing. For instance, "B" will head for the top of the key with expectations of receiving, if not the first pass, surely the next one. Each man breaks for a set up near the goal.

Set your players on the court in these positions and have them at the "Break" call out, perform the drill and put the shot up. Rotate each of the team players through each position until they understand how each position works. Every player should be capable of taking any of the positions and making it work.

Team Offensive Formations.

Team offensive formations are fundamental basketball, which is a form of controlled basketball. The upshot of this is called the "set" plays of basketball. "Set" plays offer a higher degree of success and a minimum of errors and mistakes. The players also seem to pass and handle the ball better when they know what to expect from their formations. What has developed is the 2-3, 3-2 or 1-3-1 formations which are spread out to allow movement and penetration options.

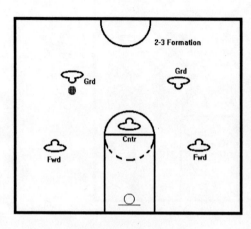

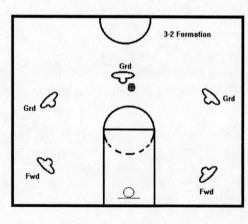

There exists a litany of "set" plays which evolve from these formations and are employed from high school through the pro's. What I've done in the following is to show some of the basic "set" plays and how they unfold during play. What I want from you and your team is to have you expand upon these plays by adding picks and screening moves.

Set up double screens and have the team walk through the positions of the players. Design your own "set" plays with your team from these basics and have fun. Get everyone involved so that the plays become theirs. Begin building from the elementary "give and go" or "pick and roll" plays then expand outward.

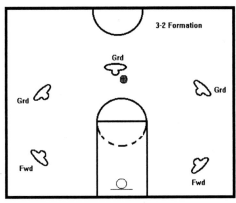

You might begin by setting half of your players into a defensive 2-3 formation. The other players shall be offense, and with a basic plan in mind, try to score. The ball is always returned to the team that is playing offense. Offense must practice faking the other players to move the ball around. Remember "fake a pass to make a pass" from the previous chapter.

Give and go is an effective two man offensive attack that usually has very good results that can beat a defense quickly. It can be carried off with either a guard and a forward or two guards from high post.

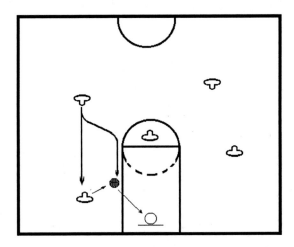

This requires two players who know each others movements to a "T". An example would be the guard passing to the forward, fakes going toward him then breaks for the basket. The forward bounce passes to the guard for a lay-up. This is pure team basketball.

One of the tricks used here is when you have an opponent who plays the ball, is to fake a pass causing him to commit himself, then get rid of the ball. This allows you to break for the return pass and lay-up.

Basic Pick and Roll

Pick and roll is a favorite in the pros. In effect it is the same as a give and go maneuver where one man sets a screen or pick at the top of the lane. He effects defense by closing the front door and appearing to be set for a pass. The passer moves laterally towards the forward drawing the defense towards the strong side. This allows the pick to roll away from his man and go for a bounce pass and a lay-up. The roll out can be in either direction.

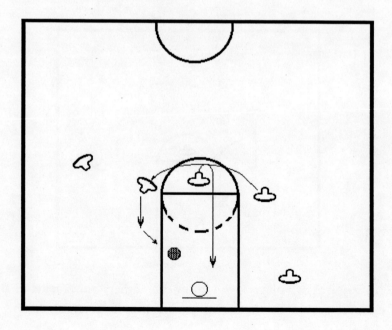

Shuffle cut-misdirection by feint with option to change.

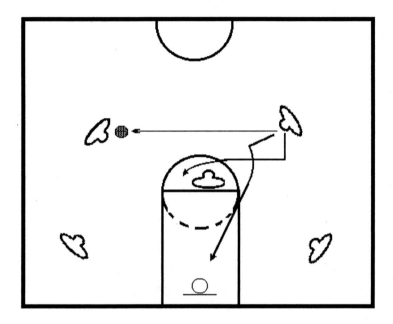

This is a play off of the high post with either the Center or a Forward positioned at the top of the key. One Guard passes to the second Guard moving in his direction, then cuts behind the high post man for a return pass. The other option to is feint towards the basket, using the high post man as a pick, cut in front of him for a return pass for the lay-up.

He can now drive the lane or option to pass off to a team player who is outside the key in the low post area. The key to this type of "set play" is speed of execution. The Guards should not hold on to the ball to long with dribbling. During instruction of the play, have all of your participants in motion. Get the team used to breaking away from the defense.

Slice around post-Single break to lane

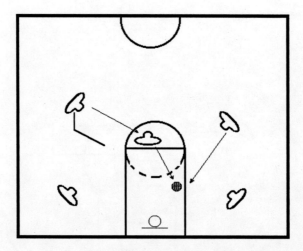

This again is a play off of the high post with either the Center or a Forward in the lane position. The Guard with the ball passes to the high post man. At the same time as the pass is made, the other Guard heads straight towards the basket from his outside position. The Guard who gave up the ball feints going for a return. The high post man however pivots and bounce passes to the Guard heading for the basket and a lay-up.

The basic floor pattern illustrated in this play option is known as the (3-2) offensive pattern. That is three across the top of the key and two outside players at mid to low post positions. The men at low post are in position to set picks or screens. They are also in position to box out for the rebound. Offensive rebounding is still a very necessary part of the play.

Slice around post-Two above high post crisscross.

This again is a play off of the high post with either the Center or a Forward in the lane position. The Guard with the ball passes to the high post man. At the same time as the pass is made, the other Guard feints going towards the basket, then cuts above and around the high post man cutting in the direction of the basket. The Guard who gave up the ball does just the opposite, cutting around high post in the other direction.

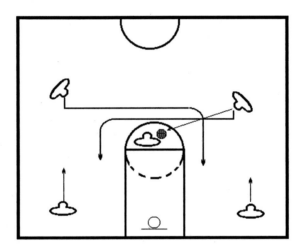

High post man has two options. He can pivot and pass to either of the Guards, or pivot and break inside the lane for a lay-up. If the Guards head for the corners, defense is pulled from high post, allowing for a one on one break.

Back Door by Forward.

Back door plays are developed to be played out along baseline and may be done by any number of means. In this case, what we want to do is use the Forward cutting to the Guard, then reversing in the direction of the basket.

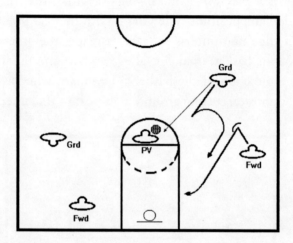

The Guard, upon passing to high post, moves to cut around high post as if heading for a return pass. At that point high post pivots to pass to the Forward who has reversed direction and receives the ball at low post. With the Guard moving forward after release of the ball, ends up in position to set a pick for the man covering the Forward going for a lay up.

The other Forward at low post is in an excellent position to go for the rebound on his side. If he gets a rebound his options are to put it up, or pass it outside for a Guard.

Slice Play: Guard & Forward on strong side.

This play calls for the passer to hit the pivot man on high post from the dribble, feint, then cut behind the forward who faked one direction then sets a pick or screen for the Guard to get around. This develops into a back door play with the Guard hitting from the side or corner. Many of these plays are a variation on a basic theme. Give and Go.

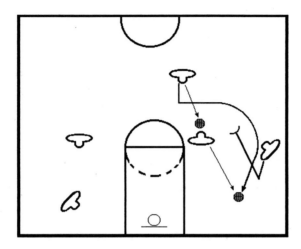

We can again recall that seventy percent of all shots made from one side of the goal, bounce to the opposite side of the hoop. Side shots are the hardest to make for the majority of players. Therefore the forward on the opposite side is in good position to either rush or attempt to box out and get the rebound.

It still remains the shooters responsibility to follow the ball in after making his shot. You always follow your shot in.

Clear out for Pivot Man

The pivot man is usually the Center, and a player who invariably can shoot in close to the basket. He is also the player who runs in, across, around and through the key.

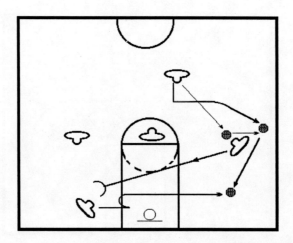

He can post up high, mid or low and get the ball back outside. What we're doing here is breaking a Forward to low post and setting a screen allowing the pivot man an escape across the key to receive a pass and put it up. Now the Forward who has cut to the low post is again on the opposite side of the hoop and in a good rebounding position.

The man at the top of the key has the option to break into the key and go for a rebound or set a pick. All players are involved in this type of play. Every man must be in motion and available to get a pass or block a turnover.

Rotational Offensive Pattern:

The most effective formation against zone defense is the 1-3-1 formation according to the experts. This sets up the "wheel", "revolve" or "whirlpool" formation which is a form of rotation around the high post. All players are moving except the low post outside man.

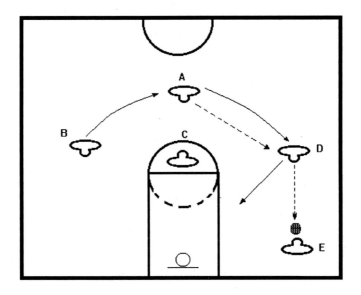

As an example, "A" will pass to "D" and the ball then going to "E" in the corner who cuts forward for a shot from the side. However if he is being played closely "D" has the option to cut in for a lay-up as a simple give and go situation. It may also develop that as "D" cuts for the basket, he will get a return pass from "E" for a lay-up.

The formation is in motion and "A" is now in the position where "D" was, "D" has cut through the lane and is now in the position or where "B" was and "B" is where "A" had been.

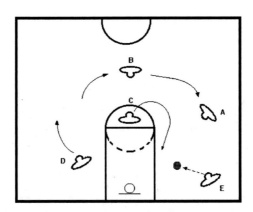

Assume the lane becomes blocked by defense, "C" now feints and cuts around toward "E" going for the basket and a pass from "E". If this does not develop "E" passes to "A", then "A" passes to "B" who passes to "D" as "C" sets a screen for the shot.

This is aggressive basketball involving a great deal of motion by all participants. You'll see this appear a lot when you are watching basketball on television College and Pro's work this kind of play a lot. I know it's beyond the abilities of the children you are coaching but it doesn't hurt for them to be shown what the more advanced players are doing. You might try some of this with you players who are at the eighth grade level.

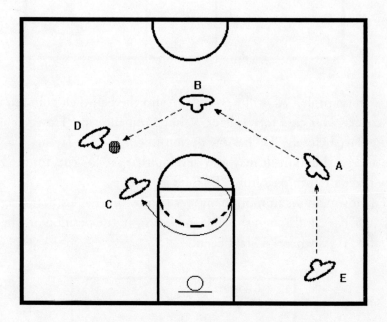

When you examine this revolving formation, you can easily see that "E" holds the key for its success. The 1-3-1 formation has remained in tact under constant movement. By doing so, they have a variety of shot possibilities which they are able to switch to. This "set" play can easily be flipped over and the corner man can be on the opposite side.

This formation can be taught to your more experienced and capable players. Have them walk through the formation and its changes while moving the ball around. Have each player stop at the points where I've indicated on the sketch and move the ball around. Do all three positions. When they know where they are going and what they are supposed to do, have them jog through the routine, feinting and passing.

Work on this during every practice with your older players until they make the play their own. Encourage speed, feinting, pivoting and going for the pass. Four or five minutes of drill time during each practice can have big dividends for the team. All team members must participate.

Jump Ball Tactics.

Some refer to the jump ball as a "tap" play. Either way, it is when the referee throws up the center ball and the team centers try to put the ball to one of their own players. There are basically two formations used in this situation, one is offensive for the team that expects to get the ball and one that is defensive for the team who doesn't expect to get the ball.

We will consider two formations, the box for offense and the 1-1-1-2 for defense. There are other formations you can use when you can be certain of controlling the tap, but at this level of play they can more or less be ignored.

The Offensive Box Formation.

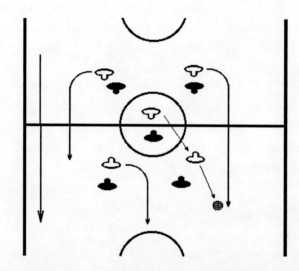

You put your tallest player in the center to try and control the tap of the ball. Next, try to get a miss match in your favor against the other teams players. The preceding diagram illustrates better than a written description of how to arrange your players. Assume that you get the ball, your opponents have placed themselves between the receiver and the basket.

Your advantage comes from the center being able to break down court between the defenders unless screened effectively by his jump opponent. The backcourt men go into a "fast break" opening up the court for lay-up opportunities.

The Defensive 1-1-1-2 Formation.

For the jump ball or tap play, you may place your men anywhere you feel they should be played. There are going to be a lot of times when your kids will be long on talent and short on tall. When you go into this formation you are conceding your ability to get the ball in the jump.

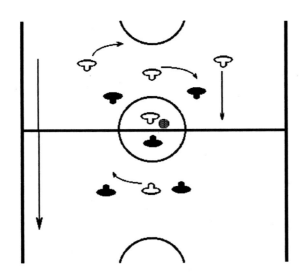

Assume your opponents have managed to gain ball possession, the defense has enough men back to protect the basket. The possibility of stealing the ball or double teaming the player with the ball has opened up for some defensive leverage. It is safe to assume that you would have your big men playing back for the added protective they provide.

Do's and Don'ts:

If clear during a rebound, use the fast break and long pass.

The Point Guard should change pace when setting up shot or pass

Always look at the basket and focus on the rim before you shoot.

Find your highest percentage shot range and polish it.

Do not force your shots or shoot when out of balance.

Learn to use the backboard for difficult angle shots.

If missing your shots, adjust for range or ball arc.

Soft shots have a better chance of bouncing in when the arc is good.

Advance the ball with a minimum of dribbling when possible.
Do not dribble into heavy traffic, get the ball to an open man.
When possible, avoid crosscourt or lob passes.
Always protect the ball with your body.
Avoid getting trapped in the corners or along the sidelines.
Do not dribble to far in front of your body, defense will steal it.

Chapter 14

Selecting Player Positions

Height and ability certainly play a part in determining where your players will be assigned positions. It stands to reason that you will want your taller men closer to the basket for both offense and defense. Shot blocking and rebounding near the basket comes with their height. They also post up well on offense.

"Well, what about the shorter players?" you ask. Don't worry about them, they are usually your best ball handlers. Not only that, they have a great deal of quickness for passing the ball around and getting it to the open man. It's hard for a tall man to steal a ball from a short player that dribbles close to the floor. The beauty of this game is that everyone has a place in it.

Your assignments break down to the Center or Centers, Forwards, Guards, Utility Players, Team Captain and Team Co-Captain. Utility players are those players who can be either a Guard or a Forward. You will have this happen quite often when you are rotating players in and out of the game. Your pivot man will most likely be your Center or a Forward. It's your bigger players who must control the lane or key.

Usually the Point Guard becomes the Team Captain. It is his job to be the floor coach and quickly assign the matching up of his team players against the other team. He is responsible for relaying signals from you to the team for set plays. He also has the option of selecting the set play and calling for a time-out if need be.

Some coaches call for Power Forwards, shooting Guards, etc. Don't bother with that in this age group. You're not being scouted by the local high school or college. Keep it simple, keep it fun. All of the above generally holds true whether we are coaching kids in **Category I** or **Category IV**. With **Category I & II**, you must physically place the players where you want them to go so that they understand their positions when play or scrimmage begins. Each player should have his place in the formation defined by you.

Secondly it gives him an identity with the team in knowing he has an assigned position with a title. There is a pride thing with youngsters in being able to say, "I'm a Forward! What are you?" Now he has defined his role as a player and as a member of a team.

So, tall is close to the backboard and basket, and also covers the key. Shorter players are your outside men who make the outside shots in most cases.

Chapter 15

Scheduling Players during games

The scheduling of players time on the court during a game is based on several factors. One is the player fairness factor, wherein everyone should have an equal amount of time on the floor during a game. If all things are equal, that is the ideal for us to follow. You also have a fairness to the team factor to consider. When under pressure during a game you must place your best players on the court during the last quarter.

Most teams will divide their players along an ability line. When setting up your schedule, try to balance the on court team with a mix of strong and weak players. This forces the weaker player to make more of an effort to do his share. It's far more motivating to the weaker player to improve, than if you sat him on the bench and let others play. Your league rules may also require you to play every player at least a quarter of the game.

If that is the case, and you feel that you have enough weak players to undermine the teams efforts, this creates a dilemma. Now you are faced with weak and strong quarters and how do you juggle that on the schedule. Well, you don't have to play an individual for a full quarter at a time. You have options in scheduling.

Look at it this way, you have four quarters to play. Instead of seeing quarters, break them in half and see eighths. Now you can fold them into play based upon eighths. Cycling them in and out for short periods of time also allows you a chance to instruct them with what you want done.

Ten Man Rotation Schedule

Quarters	1st		2nd		3rd		4th	
1	X	X			X	X		X
2			X	X			X	X
3	X	X			X	X		
4			X		X		X	
5	X	X		X				X
6		X	X		X	X		
7	X			X	X			X
8		X	X		X	X		
9	X			X	X			X
10			X	X		X	X	

Let's say you have ten players. That means you have an on court play ratio of 5 players x 8=40 player eighths. Now if I divide my 40 by ten, the number of players on the team, I get 4 eighths or half the game for each player.

How you rotate the players into the game becomes the key for the schedule. I've tried to show how flexible scheduling can become, and how you can balance the strong and weak players on court using eighths. So what we do is play the weaker player an eighth here, one there and another somewhere else. Spreading his court time allows versatility.

Another technique you have available is the substitution of players in and out for a period of a one or two plays. You can do this successfully with players who are very weak without effecting the teams ability to win.

I use this method when I feel that the player is marginal and has accrued his quarter which is the best I can give him. He gets his quarter, then in and out as a sub for a couple of additional plays.

It's only fair to allow your better players who work hard to have additional time on the court. It also motivates all players to make more of an effort in order to get more time. There is also a psychological bonus here. Rotation of the team members in and out makes them feel as if they were playing most of the game. When on the bench they are focused on the game, and this mentally extends their participation.

As your program progresses, try to make sure that no player plays less than three eighths. Remember, this is training for children, not winning for adults. I've had great success in not allowing a poor player to hide on the bench simply because he didn't play that well.

What if you had only eight players, then what? Again the 40 player eighths is divided by 8 and looks like this 40/8 = 5. That is pretty good. Now you can vary player loading from a minimum of three eighths to five eighths or three quarters.

Suggested Eight Player Schedule

Quarter	1st		2nd		3rd		4th	
1			X	X		X		X
2	X	X	X			X	X	
3	X	X	X		X	X	X	X
4			X	X	X	X	X	
5	X	X		X	X			X
6			X	X		X		X
7	X	X		X	X		X	X
8	X	X			X		X	

Chapter 16

Game Statistics

Well, by now I'm sure you've come to the conclusion that being a coach can be fun for everyone. With a little organization, some help from the parents, you are able to put a program together for your entire team. Now is the time you need to know the value of keeping game statistics on player performances during a game.

I personally keep them, but they are not for publication to either the parents or the players. They are used as a guide for training. They tell me where the team is weak and where it is strong. Statistics can be an indicator of who is playing as a team member and who isn't. It also gives me an overview of what combination of players on the floor produce the best team results.

Most coaches would conclude that the most important data is who is making the most points in the games. But it's much more than that. Who is effective in rebounding? How about foul shot percentages? Who is making the steals in defense? For a player to be able to make a shot, it is the effort of the entire team to set up the situation. Look at assists and look at turnovers.

Keep track of all shooting efforts and their results in order to see who has what kind of a scoring percentage. If the percentage is high, then you can conclude that the player is putting the ball up when he has his best shot possibility. I always tell every member of the team to shoot when they have a good opportunity of making the shot work.

It does two things. It gets the ball up, and I've taken the responsibility for the shot if it fails. The player was only doing what I had demanded of him. Put it up when you have a good shot.

Most of the teams turnovers will be from poor passing under pressure while on the court. Next they will come from poor ball handling. This again gives you the indicator of what you need the team to work on. It also points out which of the players need the most help in these areas so you can give them special drills. If the players during offensive rebounding are in close to the backboard, but unsuccessful in putting it back up for a goal, I give them a drill to help them focus on using the backboard.

The ball hog suffers from what I call "I" problems. I, I, me, me. Hey look at me! I can do it all by myself. I'm the STAR! This is usually the player with the greatest number of put ups, and the least amount of score for effort. Which in turn results in turnovers that can defeat the effort of the entire team. You need to know who this player is. You must impress him with the teams need for assists and engage his cooperation in getting them. Give him that special job.

Turnovers go both ways. Are my players creating turnovers that can and do give us the ball. Is defense stealing the ball or causing enough pressure that the other team makes mistakes. Is aggressive defense making us a stronger contender? Defense is hard to play and difficult to enforce. It requires a lot of energy from the players who are really trying. Tiredness will creep in during the last quarter and you can expect your game to slow a bit.

Who is making the most assists? Keeping track of the assists is as important as who has the best shooting percentage. This is the player who has the team spirit. That does not mean to imply that the player doesn't score well also, usually they do. By having the team spirit, you find where your "set" plays can begin, and with whom.

How are we doing on rebounds? That covers both offensive and defensive rebounding. Are we boxing out or not boxing out? Who is keeping us in the game? This is information you must have! You need it to help guide your efforts with the team. If we are getting the ball well, start working on the fast break.

During a game, I have my assistant coach keep track of what each member of the team is doing while on court. That does not mean everyone at all times, but the player who has the ball. If the player puts it up, it's recorded. If he makes an assist, it's recorded. That's what you must also do. You won't be able to record every single move or attempt or rebound, but you'll acquire enough good data to help you direct your training effort.

I make a simple form with the players name and number in the left hand column. We then assign a code for each of the important functions we are interested in, then enter that to the right of the players name.

If it's put up without score, we enter a zero (0), if scored a 2 or 3 indicating the type of shot. You may enter and "F" for each foul shot taken and made or missed. You and your assistant must devise your own codes. Enter "R" for rebounding, or "OR" for offensive rebounding and "DR" for defensive rebounding. Make it something you can use for good analysis of your teams efforts.

At the end of each quarter, draw a vertical line indicating that the quarter was completed. Now you have information on how well you were performing during that quarter as a team and how each player on court performed. Remember, you are cycling your players in and out of the game. I also keep my teams score and the other teams score by quarters at the bottom of the page.

By having a record of how you cycled the players, and the stats for the game, you can begin to focus in on where training efforts must be made. I know you are doing your best during practice scrimmages to detect where you need improvement, but this is a quantum leap ahead. It is absolutely necessary in training a good team to play as a team.

I would caution you not to use this information to intimidate a player who isn't playing well to play better. I also caution against using the statistics to put only the best players on the floor and overlook the less skilled ones. Do use it to balance the team on court during a game. Mix strong and weak allowing all of the players their fair share of playing time.

If there were to be an exception, it would be during a finals playoff where the team really needs a win. Under these conditions, no one hugging the bench is going to complain about winning. It has taken everyone's efforts to get there, and they are ready to play their best men against another team.

One thing you'll discover is some of whom you believe are your better players, seem to disappear in the stats. You know the player is doing his job, but isn't showing up in the information. What you do then is watch the player during a game. You may find he is boxing out well on defense, running the offense into traps, works as a pivot on offense and moving the ball around to others very well.

The players who seem to generate little data during a game, play like the devil during practice and scrimmage. They are playing among friends, and are relaxed while having fun. However in a game, they become shy and seek out the job which they can do best and not become a focal point of the games scrutiny. Don't worry about him, by seasons end, he'll show up big time.

I guess in summary we should say that keeping statistics during a game is one of your better tools for designing you practices and outlining your game plans. You game plans will be scheduling your players on court and the strategies you will have to employ.

Chapter 17

Basic Rules of The Game

It's my assumption that any book dealing with coaching a game should include some of, if not all of the rules pertaining to that game. Therefore, I've included those rules which have to do directly with the player when on court. I have not included the rules which regulate court size, equipment, officials and their duties, the scoring and timing regulations, etc.

It is our responsibility to teach the young players acceptable on-court behavior. What you will find here, is what you and your players will need to know in regards to playing the game fairly and understanding just what the rules and regulations are that govern the players game.

I would suggest that you don't try covering all aspects of the rules to quickly. Take your time and explain the most fundamental rules as the opportunities present themselves. Children like knowing what the rules are, and gain confidence in their play through knowing. That is a big plus for you.

CONTACT RULES

ART. I A player shall not: hold, push, charge, trip; nor impede the progress of an opponent by extending an arm, shoulder, hip or knee, or by bending the body into other than a normal position; nor use any rough tactics. He or she shall not contact an opponent with his/her hand unless such contact is only with the opponent's hand while it is on the ball and is incidental to an attempt to play the ball. The use of hands on an opponent in any way that inhibits the freedom of movement of the opponent or acts as an aid to a player in starting or stopping is not legal.

Extending the arms fully or partially other than vertically so that freedom of movement of an opponent is hindered when contact with the arms occurs is not legal. These positions are employed when rebounding, screening or in various aspects of postplay. A player may not use the forearm and hand to prevent an opponent from attacking the ball during a dribble or when throwing for goal. A player may hold the hands and arms in front of his/her face or body for protection and to absorb force from an imminent charge by an opponent.

It is a form of pushing when the player holding the ball is contacted by a defensive player who approaches from behind. Contact that is caused by the momentum of a player who has thrown for goal is a form of charging.

ART. 2 A dribbler shall not charge into nor contact an opponent in his or her path nor attempt to dribble between two opponents or between an opponent and a boundary, unless the space is such as to provide a reasonable chance for him or her to go through without contact. If a dribbler, without contact, sufficiently passes an opponent to have head and shoulders in advance of that opponent, the greater responsibility for subsequent contact is on the opponent.

If a dribbler in his/her progress is moving in a straight-line path, he or she may not be crowded out of that path, but it an opponent is able to legally obtain a defensive position in that path, the dribbler must avoid contact by changing direction or ending his/her dribble. The dribbler should not be permitted additional rights in executing a jump try for goal, pivoting, feinting or in starting a dribble.

ART. 3 A player who screens shall not:

a. When he/she is outside the visual field of a stationary opponent, take a position closer than a normal step from the opponent.

b. When he/she assumes a position at the side or in front of a stationary opponent, make contact with that opponent. It the screen is set within the visual field of a stationary opponent, the screener may be as close to the opponent as the screener desires, short of contact.

c. Take a position so close to a moving opponent that this opponent cannot avoid contact by stopping or changing direction. The speed of the player to be screened will determine where the screener may take his/her stationary position. This position will vary and may be one to two normal steps or strides from the opponent.

d. After assuming his/her legal screening position, move to maintain it, unless he or she moves in the same direction and path of the opponent. When both opponents are moving in exactly the same path and same direction, the player behind is responsible if contact is made because the player in front slows up or stops and the player behind overruns his/her opponent.

If the screener violates any of these provisions and contact results, he or she has committed a personal foul.

A player who is screened within his/her visual field is expected to avoid contact by going around the screener. In cases of screens outside the visual field, the opponent may make inadvertent contact with the screener and if the opponent is running rapidly, the contact may be severe.

Such a case is to be ruled as incidental contact provided the opponent stops or attempts to stop on contact and moves around the screen, and provided the screener is not displaced if he or she has the ball. A player may not use the arms, hands, hips or shoulders to force his/her way through a screen or to hold the screener and then push the screener aside· in order to maintain a guarding position on an opponent.

PENALTY: Personal Foul Offender is charged with one foul, and if it is his/her fifth foul (personal and technical) or if it is flagrant, he or she is disqualified.

FREE THROW RULES
SECTION 1. FREE THROW ADMINISTRATION

ART. 1 When a free throw is awarded, the administering official shall take the ball to the free-throw line of the offended team and place it at the disposal of the free thrower. A specific procedure is used to prevent delay in resuming play following a time-out or intermission. The timer will sound the authorized warning signal and final signal. The administering official will then sound the whistle to indicate play will resume.

In each situation:

a. The ball shall be handed to the free thrower if ready or it shall be placed on the floor.

b. The free-throw count shall begin and either or both teams may be charged with a violation.

c. Following a violation by one or by both teams, if that team(s) continues to delay it is a technical foul.

ART. 2 If the ball is to become dead when the last free throw for a specific penalty is not successful, players shall not occupy any spaces along the free-throw lane.

ART. 3 During a free throw when lane spaces may be occupied:

a. Each of the lane spaces adjacent to the end line shall be occupied by one opponent of the free thrower unless the resuming of play procedure is in effect.

b. A teammate of the free thrower is entitled to the next adjacent lane space on each side and to each other alternate position along each lane line.

c. Not more than one player may occupy any part of a marked lane space.

d. Only the marked lane spaces may be occupied.

ART. 4 Any player, other than the free thrower, who does not occupy , a lane space must be behind the free-throw line extended and behind the three-point line.

SECTION 2. ATTEMPTING PERSONAL-FOUL FREE THROWS.

The free throw(s) awarded because of a personal foul shall be attempted by the offended player. If such player must withdraw because of an injury or disqualification, his/her substitute shall attempt the throw(s) unless no substitute is available, in which case any teammate may attempt the throw(s).

SECTION 3. ATTEMPTING TECHNICAL-FOUL FREE THROWS.

The free throws awarded because of a technical foul may be attempted by any player of the offended team, including an entering substitute who is replacing a player or designated starter. The coach or captain shall designate the free thrower(s).

SECTION 4. TEN SECOND LIMIT.

The try for goal shall be made within 10 seconds after the ball has been placed at the disposal of the free thrower at the free-throw line. This shall apply to each free throw.

SECTION 5. RESUMING PLAY WITH THROW-IN.

After a free throw which is not followed by another free throw, the ball shall be put in play by a throw-in:

ART. 1 As after a field goal, if the try is for a personal foul other than intentional or flagrant, and is successful.

ART. 2 By any player of the free-thrower's team from out of bounds at the division line on the side opposite the scorers' and timers' table if the free throw is for a technical foul.

ART. 3 By any player of the free-thrower's team from the out-of-bounds spot nearest the foul if the free throw is for an intentional personal foul or flagrant personal foul.

SECTION 6. RESUMING PLAY DIFFERENCES.

ART. 1 If a free throw for a personal foul, other than intentional or flagrant, is unsuccessful, or if there is a multiple throw for a personal foul(s) and the last free throw is unsuccessful, the ball remains live.

ART. 2 If there is a multiple throw and both a personal and technical foul are involved, the tries shall be attempted in the order in which the related fouls were called, and it the last try is for a technical foul, or intentional or flagrant personal ``foul, the ball shall be put in play by a throw-in.

SECTION 7.PENALTY ADMINISTRATION-SEQUENCE.

Penalties for fouls are administered in the order in which the fouls occurred. **Question-**Two free throws are awarded to A1 and before the clock starts, two free throws are awarded to B for a technical foul on the coach of Team A. What is the correct procedure? **Answer-**With no players lined up, A1 shall attempt his/her two free throws and Team B shall attempt its two free throws, after which the ball is awarded to Team B out of bounds at the division line on the side opposite the scorers' table.

VIOLATIONS AND PENALTIES RULES
SECTION 1. FREE THROW PROVISIONS:

A player shall not violate the following provisions governing free throws.

ART. 1 The try shall be attempted from within the free throw semicircle and behind the free-throw line.

ART. 2 An opponent of the fee thrower shall occupy each lane space adjacent to the end line during the try unless the resuming of play procedure is in effect and no teammate of the free thrower may occupy either of these lane spaces.

After the ball is placed at the disposal of a free thrower:

ART. 3 He/she shall throw within 10 seconds, and in such a way that the ball enters the basket or touches the ring before the free throw ends.

ART. 4 The free thrower shall not fake a try, nor shall any player in a marked lane space fake to cause an opponent to violate.

ART. 5 No opponent shall disconcert the free thrower.

ART. 6 No player shall enter or leave a marked lane space.

ART. 7 The free thrower shall not have either foot beyond the vertical plane of the edge of the free-throw line which is farther from the basket or the free- throw semicircle line.

ART. 8 A player, other than the free thrower, who does not occupy a marked lane space, may not have either foot beyond the vertical plane of the free- throw line extended and the three-point line which is farther from the basket.

ART. 9 A player occupying a marked lane space may not have either foot beyond the vertical plane of the outside edge of any lane boundary, or beyond the vertical plane of any edge of the space (2 inches by 36 inches) designated by a lane-space mark or beyond the vertical plane of any edge of the space (12 inches by 36 inches) designated by a neutral zone.

NOTE: The restrictions in Articles 6 through 9 apply until the ball touches the ring or backboard or until the free throw ends.

PENALTY: (Section 1)

1. If the violation is by the free thrower or a teammate only, the ball becomes dead when the violation occurs and no point can be scored by that throw:

a. If the violation occurs during a free throw for a personal foul, other than intentional or flagrant, the ball is awarded to the opponents for a throw-in from the designated out-of-bounds spot nearest the violation.

b. It the violation occurs during a free throw for a technical foul, the ball is awarded to the thrower's team for a throw-in at the division line on the side of the court opposite the scorers' and timers' table.

c. If the violation occurs during a free throw for a flagrant personal foul or an intentional personal foul, the ball is awarded to the thrower's team for a throw-in from the designated out-of-bounds spot nearest the foul.

2. It the violation is by the free-thrower's opponent only:

a. If the try is successful, the goal counts and the violation is disregarded.

b. If the try is not successful, the ball becomes dead when the free throw ends, and a substitute throw shall be attempted by the same free thrower under conditions the same as for the free throw for which it is substituted.

3. If there is a violation by each team, the ball becomes dead when the violation by the free-thrower's team occurs, no point can be scored and play shall be resumed by the team entitled to the alternating-possession throw-in from the designated out-of-bounds spot nearest to where the double violation occurred.

The out-of-bounds provision in penalty item (1) and the throw-in provision in penalty item (3) do not apply if the free throw is to be followed by another free throw. In penalty item (3), if a violation by the free thrower follows disconcertion, a substitute free throw shall be awarded. In penalty item (3), if a fake by an opponent causes a teammate of the free thrower to violate, only the fake is penalized.

SECTION 2. THROW-IN PROVISIONS

A player shall not violate the following provisions governing the throw-in. The thrower shall not:

ART. 1 Leave the designated throw-in spot until the ball has been released on a throw-in pass.

ART. 2 Fail to pass the ball directly into the court so it touches or is touched by another player (inbounds or out of bounds) on the court before going out of bounds untouched.

ART. 3 Pass the ball so it is touched by a teammate while the ball is on the out-of-bounds side of the throw-in boundary-line plane.

ART. 4 Consume five seconds from the time the throw-in starts until the ball is released on a pass directly into the court.

ART. 5 Carry the ball onto the court.

ART. 6 Touch the ball in the court before it touches or is touched by another player.

ART. 7 Throw the ball so it enters the basket before it touches or is touched by another player.

ART. 8 Throw the ball so it lodges between the backboard and ring or comes to rest on the flange before it touches or is touched by another player.

No player shall:

ART. 9 Replace the thrower after the ball is at the thrower's disposal.

ART 10 Be out of bounds when he or she touches or is touched by the ball after it has been released on a throw-in pass.

Furthermore:

ART I I The opponent(s) of the thrower shall not have any part of his/her person through the inbound side of the throw-in boundary-line plane until the ball has been released on a throw-in pass.

NOTE: The thrower may penetrate the plane provided he or she does not touch the inbound area before the ball is released on the throw-in pass. The opponent in this situation may legally touch or grasp the ball. See penalty.

ART. 12 No teammate of the thrower shall be out of bounds after a designated-spot throw-in begins.

PENALTY: (Section 2) The ball becomes dead when the violation or technical foul occurs. Following a violation, the ball is awarded to the opponents for a throw-in at the out-of-bounds spot nearest the violation. (Article 11 only):

1. The first violation of the throw-in boundary-line plane by an opponent(s) of the thrower shall result in a team warning for delay being given (one warning per team per game). The warning does not result in the loss of the opportunity to move along the end line when and if applicable.

2. The second or additional violations will result in a technical foul assessed to the offending team.

3. If an opponent(s) of the thrower reaches through the throw-in boundary-line plane and touches or dislodges the ball, a technical foul shall be charged to the offender. No warning for delay required.

4. If an opponent(s) of the thrower reaches through the throw-in boundary-line plane and fouls the thrower, an intentional personal foul shall be charged to the offender. No warning for delay required.

SECTION 3. OUT OF BOUNDS
A player shall not cause the ball to go out of bounds.

Question-The dribbler steps on or outside a boundary, but does not touch the ball while he or she is out of bounds. Is this a violation? **Answer**-Yes.

SECTION 4. TRAVEL, KICK, FIST
A-player shall not run (travel) with the ball, intentionally kick it, strike it with the fist or cause it to enter and pass through the basket from below.

NOTE: Kicking the ball is a violation only when it is a positive act; accidentally striking the ball with the foot or leg is not a violation.

SECTION 5. DOUBLE DRIBBLE
A player shall not dribble a second time after his/her first dribble has ended, unless it is after he or she has lost control because of:

ART. 1 A try for field goal.

ART. 2 A bat by an opponent.

ART. 3 A pass or fumble which has then touched, or been touched by, another player.

SECTION 6. JUMP BALL
A player shall not violate any provision of the jump ball. If both teams simultaneously commit violations during the jump ball or if the referee makes a bad toss, the toss shall be repeated.

SECTION 7. THREE SECONDS.

A player shall not remain for three seconds in that part of his/her free-throw lane between the end line and the farther edge of the free-throw line while the ball is in control of his/her team in his/her frontcourt. Allowance shall be made for a player who, having been in the restricted area for less than three seconds, dribbles in or moves to try for goal. The count shall not begin or it shall be terminated during an interrupted dribble.

Question-Does the three-second restriction apply to a player who has only one foot touching the lane boundary? **Answer**-Yes. The line is part of the lane. All lines designating the free-throw lane, but not lane-space marks and neutral-zone marks, are part of the lane.

NOTE: The three seconds may vary in time from four to five.

SECTION 8. TEN SECONDS

A player shall not be, nor may his/her team be, in continuous control of a ball which is in his/her backcourt for 10 seconds.

SECTION 9. BACKCOURT

A player shall not be the first to touch a ball which is in team control after it has been in the frontcourt, if he or she or a teammate last touched or was touched by the ball in the frontcourt before it went to the backcourt.

EXCEPTION 1: it is not a violation when after a jump ball or a throw-in, a player is the first to secure control of the ball while both feet are off the floor and he or she then returns to the floor with one or both feet in the backcourt.

EXCEPTION 2: it is not a violation it a defensive player who jumped from frontcourt, secures control of the ball while both feet are off the floor and he or she returns to the floor with one or both feet in backcourt.

NOTE: It a player of the team in control in its backcourt causes the ball to go from backcourt to frontcourt and return to backcourt in team control without touching a player in frontcourt, it is a violation for such player or teammate to be first to touch it there.

SECTION 10. CLOSELY GUARDED

ART. 1 A player shall not while closely guarded:

a. Anywhere in his/her frontcourt, hold the ball for five seconds or dribble the ball for five seconds.

b. In his/her frontcourt, control the ball for five seconds in an area enclosed by screening teammates.

ART. 2 A closely-guarded count shall not be started during an interrupted dribble.

ART. 3 A closely-guarded count shall be terminated during an interrupted dribble.

PENALTY: (Sections 3 through 10) **The ball becomes dead or remains dead when the violation occurs. The ball is awarded to the opponents for a throw-in from the designated out-of-bounds spot nearest the violation.**

SECTION 11. BASKET INTERFERENCE

A player shall not commit basket interference. Basket interference occurs when a player:

ART. 1 Touches the ball or basket, (including the net), when the ball is on or within either basket.

ART. 2 Touches the ball when it is touching the cylinder having the ring as its lower base.

ART. 3 Touches the ball outside the cylinder while reaching through the basket from below.

EXCEPTION: In Articles I or 2, if a player has his/her hand legally in contact with the ball, it is not a violation if such contact with the ball continues after it enters a basket cylinder or if in such action, the player touches the basket. Dunking or stuffing is legal and is not basket interference.

SECTION 12. GOALTENDING

A player shall not commit goaltending. Goaltending occurs when a player touches the ball during a field-goal try or tap while it is in its downward flight entirely above the basket ring level and has the possibility of entering the basket in flight, or an opponent of the free thrower touches the ball outside the cylinder during a free-throw attempt.

PENALTY: (Sections 11-12)

1 . If the violation is at the opponent's basket, the opponents are awarded one point if during a free throw, three points if during a three-point try and two points in any other case. The crediting of the score and subsequent procedure are the same as if the awarded score had resulted from the ball having gone through the basket, except that the official shall hand the ball to a player of the team entitled to the throw-in.

2. If the violation is at a team's own basket, no points can be scored, and the ball is awarded to the opponents for a throw-in from the designated out-of-bounds spot nearest the violation.

3. If the violation results from touching the ball while it is in the basket after entering from below, no points are scored and the ball is awarded to the opponents for a throw-in from the designated out-of-bounds spot nearest the violation.

4. If there is a violation by both teams, play shall be resumed by the team entitled to the alternating-possession throw-in at the out-of-bounds spot nearest to where the simultaneous violations occurred.

FOULS AND PENALTIES RULES

SECTION 1. TEAM TECHNICAL

A team shall not:

ART. I Fail to supply the scorer with the name and number of each squad member who may participate and designate the five starting players at least 10 minutes before the scheduled starting time.

ART. 2 After the time limit specified in Article 1:

a. Change a designated starter unless necessitated by illness, injury illegal equipment or apparel.

b. Add a name to the squad list.

c. Require the scorer to change a squad member's or player's number in the scorebook.

d. Require a player to change to the number in the scorebook.

e. Have identical numbers on squad members and/or players.

ART. 3 Use television monitoring or replay equipment or computers (other than for statistics) for coaching purposes during the game or any intermission or use a megaphone or any mechanical sounding device or any electronic transmission device at courtside for coaching purposes, or electronic equipment for voice communication with players.

ART. 4 Fail to occupy the players' bench to which it is assigned.

ART. 5 Allow the game to develop into an actionless contest, this includes the following and similar acts:

a. When the clock is not running consuming a full minute through not being ready when it is time to start either half.

b. Delay the game by preventing the ball from being made promptly live or from being put in play.

c. Contact with the free thrower or a huddle of two or more players by either team prior to a free throw following the team warning for this delay.

d. Interfering with the ball following a goal after the team warning for this delay.

ART. 6 Have more than five squad members participating simultaneously.

ART. 7 Request an excess time-out.

ART. 8 Commit an unsportsmanlike foul.

ART. 9 Fail to have all players return to the court at approximately the same time following a time-out or intermission.

ART. 10 Following the team warning for delay the thrower shall not leave the designated throw-in spot until the ball has been released or commit a violation of the throw-in boundary-line plane.

ART. I1 Allow players to lock arms or grasp a teammate) in an effort to restrict the movement of an opponent.

PENALTY: (All articles) Two free throws plus ball for division-line throw-in. (Art. 1) One foul for both requirements. (Art. 2) One foul

only per team regard. less of the number of infractions. (Art. 2a) Penalized if discovered before ball becomes live to start game. (Arts. 1, 2b, c, d) Penalized when they occur. (Art. 2e) Penalized when discovered. (Art. 6) Penalized if discovered while being violated.

Summary of Penalties for All Fouls

The offended player or team is awarded the following:

1. No free throws for:

a. Each common foul before the bonus rule is in effect.

b. A player-control foul.

c. A double personal foul.

d. A double technical foul or a simultaneous technical foul by opponents.

In c or d, an alternating-possession throw-in follows.

2. One free throw if fouled in the act of shooting and two-or three-point try or tap is successful.

3. Bonus free throw:

a. For seventh, eighth and ninth team foul each half, if first free throw is successful.

b. Beginning with 10th team foul each half whether or not first free throw is successful.

4. Two free throws if intentional or flagrant, plus ball for throw-in.

5. Fouled in act of shooting and try or tap is unsuccessful:

a. Two free throws on two-point try or tap.

b. Three free throws on three-point try or tap.

Plus ball for throw-in if intentional or flagrant.

6. Multiple Foul:

a. One free throw for each foul:

(1) No try involved.

(2) Successful or unsuccessful two-point try or tap.

(3) Successful three-point try or tap.

b. Two free throws for each foul:

(1) Intentional or flagrant foul.

(2) Unsuccessful three-point try or tap.

Plus ball for throw-in if intentional or flagrant.

7. In case of a false double foul or a false multiple foul, each foul carries its own penalty.

Question (1)-A guard moves into the path of a dribbler and contact occurs. Who responsible? **Answer**-Either may be responsible, but greater responsibility is that of the dribbler if the guard conforms to the following principles which officials use in reaching a decision. The guard is assumed to have obtained a guarding position if he or she is in the dribbler's path facing him or her. If he or she jumps into position, both feet must return to the floor after the jump before he or she has obtained a guarding position No specific stance or distance is required. It is assumed the guard may shift to maintain his/her position in the path of the dribbler, provided he or she does not charge into the dribbler nor otherwise cause contact.

The responsibility of the dribbler for contact is not shifted merely because the guard turns or ducks to absorb shook when contact by the dribbler is imminent. The guard may not cause by moving under or in front of passer or thrower after he or she is the air with both feet off the floor.

Question (2)-One or both fouls of either a multiple foul or a double personal foul are flagrant. What is the procedure? **Answer**-For a multiple foul, two free throws are awarded for each flagrant foul. For a double personal foul, no free throws are awarded. In either case, any player who commits a flagrant foul is disqualified.

Question (3)-Does the goal count it the ball goes into the basket after a foul? **Answer**-Yes, unless the ball becomes dead before it enters the basket or the goal is canceled.

Well that should give you a fairly good run-down on how the game is played. All of these rules have been around a long time, and aren't as subject to change as uniform codes, logo's, numbers or names. When we see the NBA in action, you wonder if any of them are invoked. They are, but there is an awful lot of physical motion going on.

With children, aggression is viewed in many ways, with these rules in place, you can prevent a lot of injuries and hurt feelings. We are the ones who have the honor of teaching them how to play the game.

About the Author

An Engineer, writer and author. Life long sports fan and for more than thirty years a volunteer coach in sports. During this period of time I have also shown new coaches how to plan, schedule and rotate their players during game. Teaching how to coax the best from the players without pushing the player.

Printed in the United States
2975